Divided

A Memoir Of A Family I Never Knew

Published by Double A Publishing 2024.

Contact

Email: abneyandrew81@gmail.com

Facebook: https://www.facebook.com/profile.php?id=61561318201455

Dedication

This book is dedicated to Darlene Mazon because without her this book may not have ever been written. She opened my eyes and gave me the courage to pursue answers to questions that plagued me my entire life. Although she was confined to a wheelchair she stood up straight for what she believed in. She encouraged me to find the truth no matter where it took me.

Table of Contents

Foreword

If you want to ruin or awaken your life simply order a DNA test kit and wait for the results to come back. People take DNA tests for various reasons. Some think it's cool to find out their family heritage while others are searching for something more. For me it was to find the truth of who was my biological father. Whatever your reasons are prepare yourself before you go down that road because the truth you thought may not be the truth you find or was looking for.

In this book, you are not merely a reader but a witness to the personal journey of someone who has chosen to peel back the layers and offer a raw, unvarnished view of their world. This is my story of salvation and redemption and how one day a phone call suddenly changed my life forever.

My story is common yet unique. My story speaks to millions of people who thought their lives and upbringings were dysfunctional but came to find out that their life was quite common as compared to others in similar situations.

There is something profoundly powerful about stories that come from lived experience. They remind us that while our paths may differ, the essence of what we seek-purpose, connection, and meaning-remains universal. As you turn the pages of this book, prepare to be moved, inspired, and perhaps, see your own story reflected in the narrative. This is not just the author's tale, but a reminder that we all carry within us stories worth telling. In this memoir, truth and vulnerability are the guides. May it stir something within you.

The Beginning

When we are born two of the most powerful feelings I believe we experience is love and rejection. Those two feelings will have a powerful impact on you for the rest of your life and how you manage them will determine the direction of your life.

My life started in February of 1964 in Waterbury, Connecticut, a midsize town of approximately 115,000 people located southwest of Hartford, the state's capitol. Waterbury was known as the Brass Capital of the World for its high-quality brass and copper product production during the 19th century.

The identity of my biological father was something my mother never wanted to talk about for some reason. Some folks had their speculations of who my biological father was, and those speculations were surrounded around a single man, David. This was the same man whom my great grandmother had once told me when I was young was my biological father. Over the years though I had my doubts.

Before she told me who he was she said, "everyone should know who their parents are." After telling me who she believed was my biological father she made me promise not to tell anyone that she had told me. I kept that promise not to tell for the next fifty years.

My great grandmother has since passed, but little did we know that even our secret had a secret. I had already vowed to myself to never go looking for my biological father or family. Not because I didn't want to know, but because I didn't want to disrupt or hurt anyone else with this secret. Upon finding out the truth of my biological father, my story brought out a range of feelings in me that I never felt before, some that I didn't even know existed. It made me question everything I thought I ever knew about my mother and my life.

It's difficult for me to forgive my mother for not telling me the truth because before forgiveness can be given, responsibility must be accepted. Taking responsibility is something my mother has never done and probably never will. Through all of this I learned that you can't think about vengeance and do the work that needs to be done.

In order to truly know your future, you must know your past and exposing old lies can be very uncomfortable for some people.

To better understand my story, I had to track down as many people as I could and bring their stories back to life. Stories from people who are alive and stories of some who have long since passed. I made sure that their voices would be heard from the grave. My regret is for the people who have since passed. They did not get the opportunity to know the truth.

In order to know how this all started I have to start with the person who is at the center of it all, my mother, Sallie Mae Abney. My mother must have been a magician because she sure pulled off one hell of an illusion for a long time. I once heard that that the greatest illusion the Devil ever did was make people think he didn't exist. I'm not saying my mother is the Devil, but she sure knows some of his tricks.

Sallie Mae

Every story has a beginning, and this one starts with my mother. My mother was born Sallie Mae Green in March of 1940 in Saluda, South Carolina. Although she went by the name Sallie Mae Abney for most of her life, this was not her birth name. My mother's father was Willie Green. Although this was my grandfather he was a person I never heard of or knew growing up. Just like my biological father, my mother for whatever reason, chose not to tell me about him. This journey not only uncovered who my biological father, siblings and family were, it also uncovered who my grandfather and his family were.

My mother never told me anything about her father, not even his name. I just learned about my grandfather a few years ago when I did the DNA test. This might lead some people to think that maybe something bad happened between my mother and her father, but no. She was in contact with him and his family her entire life, I just wasn't included. His family knew about me, but I just didn't know about them. I don't want to get ahead of myself, so we'll get into my grandfather's story later.

My mother was one of two children born to my grandmother, Ethel Lee Allen. My grandmother was not married to either of her children's fathers at the time she gave birth to them. After her two children were born she subsequently left home to go north to start her life without them. Why did she leave her two babies behind? I'll probably never know the answer to that. I am unsure of when she left, but her marriage certificate says she was married in Waterbury, CT in 1948 to Cephus Allen.

My mother and her brother were raised by my great grandfather and great grandmother, Andrew Abney and Missie Lou Abney. Given that they raised them as their own, my mother was named after my great grandmother's mother, Sallie Mason and her brother was named after my great grandfather's father, Fred Abney.

Although my mother wasn't born an Abney my great grandparents just used their last name to keep everyone's name in the household unified. Back in those days record keeping was scarce and nobody really kept track of paperwork that closely.

My great grandmother use to tell me stories of when my mother and uncle were growing up and how mischievous my mother was. She once told me a story about how my mother was always hardheaded and constantly ignored her when she told her not to jump into the laundry basket after school. According to my great grandmother my mother would always blindly jump into the laundry basket to hide after school. My great grandmother said that in order to stop her from doing that she had killed a big black snake in the yard and put it in the basket for when my mother got home from school. According to my great grandmother my mother came home from school as usual took the lid off the basket and blindly jumped in it. The next thing you know my great grandmother said she heard my mother scream; she knew exactly what had happened. From that day on my mother never jumped into that laundry basket again.

In 1958 my mother graduated from high school in Saluda, SC. Her brother had graduated two years earlier from the same high school and was now married and living at home with his wife. Also, in 1958 my great grandfather, Andrew, passed away. By this time my grandmother, as well as several other family members, had found employment and were settled in Waterbury, CT.

Later that year my great grandmother, mother, uncle and his wife, along with their baby girl, all moved to Waterbury, CT to be with their family. This is where things become tricky. My biological father, William Lee Felton, was already living in Waterbury, CT at the time my mother and her family had arrived there. He was two years younger than my mother and graduated from high school in Waterbury, CT in 1960. Upon going to California and visiting my brother I looked in my biological father's high school yearbook that my brother had. Inside I found two of my mother's close cousins that played football and graduated with my biological father. I can't prove it, but I believe my mother knew William way before he got married in 1963. I also found out later that my mother was friends with William's younger sister and worked with his older sister at Uniroyal. My mother seemed to be well connected with his family.

My mother's penchant for keeping secrets was notoriously known. Growing up I would catch my mother lying about some of the most ridiculous things that she didn't need to lie about. Sometimes I think she would just say things without thinking and when she got caught up in them she just refused to acknowledge that what she said was not the truth. Later me and my stepfather and I would talk about this. Some of the things he told me about my mother and how she had lied to him about things throughout the years was ridiculous. Some of the lies were just absurd and uncalled for.

Another trait of my mother was talking about other people and being a busy body. This especially bothered me because I am not that kind of a person. Although my mother liked sticking her nose in other people's business you better stick your nose in hers. She was known for her fiery temper and vicious attitude which made people keep their distance. Although my mother didn't drink, smoke nor curse she still had her share of issues. Make no mistake there were and are far worse mothers than mine, I'm just saying that on the surface she presented herself as something much different than what she really was. She was always very stylish and conscious about how she presented herself to the world and would turn on that southern belle accent when needed.

In 2020 my mother had a near death episode from Covid 19. You would think having a near death episode from Covid might make her softened her stance on things, but not my mother. There's an old saying that goes "Whatever doesn't kill you makes you stronger." If that saying is true then my mother must be Wonder Woman by now.

I'm not one to believe in Karma or divine intervention but maybe my mother survived Covid so that she could be confronted by her past. Maybe that was the closure that I needed. My mother is old now, but she still hasn't lost her fiery temper. Why would she still have so much contempt for a man who has since been long gone, I don't know. Maybe it isn't contempt, maybe it's embarrassment or rejection. Either way it's unhealthy and uncalled for. Many people in our family have tried to talk to her and explain to her that I had the right to know these things, but my mother is just self-centered and all she cares about is what is best for her. My mother is a broken person, just like many of us are, but she first needs to forgive herself so that she can move on with her own life and fix whatever is left of her life.

I often wondered where my mother got her anger from. Did she grow up that way or did she become this way after meeting William? As I got to talk to my other newfound siblings I found out that my mother wasn't the only angry woman that William was involved with. Several of my siblings gave similar accounts of their mothers growing up. For me forgiveness was not necessary in order for me to move on as long as I didn't let my anger destroy me from inside. I used that anger to move forward and not look back. I made the decision to be the captain of my ship.

I sometimes wish there were something that I could do to help my mother, but I know there isn't. I take no joy in knowing she is like this, full of anger and resentment, but I also know there's nothing that I can do about it. I truly do wish her the best and hope that one day she will forgive herself and make amends.

My Childhood

was brought into this world in February of 1964, three months after President Kennedy was assassinated in Texas and during the height of the civil rights movement. Technically I was born without civil rights seeing that the act didn't become effective until July 2, 1964. I don't know if I was welcomed into this world, but I arrived here none the less. No child makes the decision to be brought into this world, that decision was made for us. Being born is like playing cards, you are dealt a hand and hopefully you get a good enough hand to play with to win. But getting a good hand doesn't mean you will always win. I have seen many people in my lifetime that had everything and then lost it all.

I grew up in a poor to middle class household. What that means is we didn't go hungry but there was very little money left over for extras. I remember things like putting plastic over the windows in the winter to keep the draft out to stay warm because the only source of heat we had was from the stove. There was a heater built into the wall in our apartment, but it rarely ever worked. I spent many cold days and nights in that house. As a child I promised myself that when I grow up I was never going to live in a cold house again. That's a promise I have kept to this day. When it came time for breakfast on school days there was no such thing as a hot breakfast. Hot breakfast was reserved for the weekends and special occasions. This also applied to any meal. There were no choices when it came to what you ate. The few times I asked my grandmother what was for dinner the answer was always the same, food. Eventually I stopped asking. My family was a bunch of hardworking people who did their best to get by on what they had.

As a child I remember hearing the word no an awful lot. If it wasn't a necessity the answer was always no. I think my childhood theme song was NO!. Can I have this, NO! Can I go there, NO! Can I get that, NO! Can I have some money, HELL NO! Coming from the south that was the way it was for them. My great grandmother told me a story one time of how she got a slice of pie and a pair of shoes for

Christmas. I just looked at her and said quietly to myself don't try that shit with me.

Christmas was my favorite time of the year. I loved Christmas so much that for a number of years I always ended up in the hospital for asthma attacks on Christmas Day. I would get so excited the night before until I would trigger an asthma attack that required a trip to the hospital on Christmas Eve. I really loved Christmas. I guess being the only child in the house had its perks. There was one time I was in the hospital's children's ward for Christmas, and they had Santa Claus come to our room and give us presents to cheer all the children up.

When I was a child I was a huge fan of Elvis Presley. I watched all his movies and knew his songs. I remember asking the nurse if they could give me a face lift so that I could look like Elvis Presley while I was there. That nurse must have thought I was crazy. An African American child wanting to look like Elvis Presley. I'm just going to go with maybe I had a fever.

I had no cell phone nor television with all the premium channels or video games. I spent most of my time growing up outside. I would be told to go outside to play and to be back before the sun went down. I remember the one time I pushed it a little too far and came back when the sun was down and all you could see was the orange glow over the horizon. My grandfather was standing at the gate waiting for me. I knew it wasn't going to be good, so I came up with something quick to say before I approached him. Out of nowhere I said, "The sun isn't completely down." He just looked at me and said, "You're pushing it. Next time I better be able to see the sun when you come home." I dodged any consequences that day, but I made sure that it never happen again. Other kids in my neighborhood were on the street light method. When the street lights came on you had better make your way into the house.

I remember standing on the street corner with friends playing a game called "That's my car." This was a game that if you saw a nice car drive by you claimed it by saying "That's my car." Being poor we knew the chances of owning any of these cars was probably not in our future, but you can't stop a kid from dreaming. When I became an adult I owned many of those cars that I thought were just a dream as a kid. Always encourage your kids to dream big, if they miss the moon they will still be amongst the stars.

We often went to the Goodwill store to shop for clothing. I remember my great grandmother sewing patches over holes in my clothes to make them last longer. There were also those cheap iron on patches that never really seemed to go on right. When it came to sneakers I could get whatever sneakers I wanted as long as they were the Uniroyal rejects that they sold in the basement of the Uniroyal factory for two or three dollars a pair. Trust me it beat wearing skips. I remember that old song, "Skips, they make your feet feel fine, Skips, they cost a dollar ninety-nine." The last thing you wanted was a bunch of kids doing a chorus around you with that song. As a child I was taught the value of a dollar and to only spend on what was necessary. I can't speak for all my siblings but I'm sure some of them may have shared similar experiences growing up.

We did, however, do annual trips to South Carolina to visit family and friends. This was a family ritual. Sometimes they would do two trips, one before the summer and one after it ended before school started. Sometimes they would leave me in South Carolina in the beginning of the summer so I could hang out with my family and pick me back up at the end of summer so I could to go back to school. Before each trip there was always the ghetto NASCAR inspection to make sure that the family car was up for the trip. Later when my family had more money they would rent a car for the trip rather than trust or put the mileage on the family car. They always saved room in the car to bring back meats, peanuts and other items that they liked which weren't available to them in the north. Those were their treats for that feeling of being back home. I used to think how sad it was that people had to leave the place that they loved and grew up at just because of the way some people treated them because of their skin color. There was also the issue of lack of job opportunities available for them. The north provided greater opportunities.

It's amazing how many jobs they had for Black people when they didn't have to pay them and the audacity of White people to blame the slave economy on their lack of employment opportunities. Did they ever think to blame the greedy business owners for their lack of employment in the south? Then to add insult to injury, when the civil war was over and slavery was abolished, White immigrants came to this country and felt they deserved employment over the Black people who had worked in this country for hundreds of years without pay and under inhumane conditions. This explains a lot of what we see going on today in this country. I believe the term they use is White Privilege.

My great grandmother was our family cook and everything she made was made from scratch. I know because I was her assistant in the kitchen doing whatever prep work she thought I was capable of doing. As I got older I became her garden assistant, turning over the soil and picking fruits and vegetable when they became ripe.

I was born on a street named Newell Place in the north end of town in Waterbury, Connecticut but by the time I became a one-year-old my family bought a three-family house and we moved to Putnam Street in Waterbury, Connecticut. Putnam Street was a predominately White neighborhood when we moved there, but by the time I became a teen it was just the hood. I experienced the same thing when I became an adult and bought my first one family house in the east end of town. I don't know if it was the minorities following the minorities or if it was the White people making an escape. Either way that's just the way it went, minorities in, Whites out.

There were a few White families that did stay in the hood. Those were the ones whose families were too poor to keep up with the other Whites. But even those Whites as they grew older seemed to do better economically than their minority counterparts from the same area. This is usually a sour subject for some White people because they think that just because they started out with us they weren't thrown a few bones along the way to help them along with their progress. They fail to recognize, or don't want to recognize, just how badly African Americans in this country were treated and abused for hundreds of years and that we are still fighting the effects and injustices of those times today. This also holds true for anyone who appears to be of African descent. They have to suffer the same racial injustices that society dishes out to us daily.

As integration started to increase segregation still continued, just in different forms. Separate but equal was just a slogan. There are those who want to keep us separate and will die before there is ever any real sense of equality in the USA. Separation of the less fortunate creates money and power for the wealthy.

Fortunately for me I was able to make a good thing out of some bad news. There were many times that I wondered if my mother ever thought or wished that she had not brought me into this world. I never heard her say it, unlike other stories where people said they did hear their mothers say that about them. I know that is a terrible thing to say, but if I'm going to be honest with myself then why pretend that it never crossed my mind? My mother never was and still isn't a loving, nurturing type of person. There were many times growing up when my mother proved this to be true, but there were three times that this really stood out.

The first was when I was in the eighth grade. When I told my mother about the eight-grade graduation her response was, "you're that old?" I don't know if she was joking but it sure didn't feel like it. The second time was when I was seventeen years old and got into a motorcycle accident. She never wanted me to ride a motorcycle and her reaction to my accident showed it. I spent a few days in the hospital after the accident and not once did my mother call or come by to see how I was doing.

The third time was when I was twenty-one years old, and I got shot as a victim of an attempted robbery. I was in the hospital for a week, and she came by to see me one time. Not to ask how I was doing but to scold me as to what was I doing to get shot. I was the victim of a random robbery attempt. Wrong place at the wrong time. I didn't even know the person. There were plenty of other times that my mother showed her coldness, but these three times always stand out to me.

My mother was living with my great grandmother when she got pregnant with me. If she did get the thought to terminate the pregnancy it would have been short-lived because my great grandmother wouldn't have gone for her not having the baby. Family was important to my great grandmother and terminating her great grandson would not have been an option. I believe it was my great grandmother's idea to name me after her late husband. Some mothers have no idea how much they can make or break their child with their life decisions.

As I found out later in life, my mother had a lot of animosity towards my biological father. After finding out who my biological father was and seeing photos of him I could see why. We shared many similar physical features. I was probably just a constant reminder to her of the man that she despised so much.

I have always been very ambitious. Since as long as I can remember I always believed I could be or do whatever I wanted to do if I put my mind to it. Life was nothing more than time and opportunity, but I wasn't totally oblivious. I knew I was an African American male in America and that meant ambitions with limitations. Equality is something we hear about, but does it truly exist? From the beginning points had already been deducted from me. I was labeled and stereotyped just because of who I was and what I represented. I was from a broken home. This isn't to say that you can't succeed in life just because you weren't dealt a perfect hand, it just meant you would have to work twice as hard to get half as much. A lot of young Black children were told growing up that they would have to work twice as hard to get half of what White people get. I truly don't believe we got half. It was more like less than half.

As Africans our identities were stripped from us as soon as we landed in this country. African people in America didn't create the environment that they lived in; it was forced upon them. They lost everything. They lost their ethnicity, their names, their culture, their religion and their freedoms. These were just a few of the things they lost.

Africans didn't create biracial children; they were created through them. I personally don't believe there is any such thing as biracial for Black people. Everyone knows if you have one ounce of Black blood in you aren't White. White Americans will not accept you as one of them.

Our problems in life were created for us a very long time ago and we still pay for them today. I say these things not to blame White people for all of the problems Black people endure, we create enough of our own problems, but without knowing this how can you honestly judge someone? This is the education they don't want children to learn in school. They don't want woke people, they want people who are walking in their sleep, obeying what they are told and never questioning anything. They want people who are able to function but not able to comprehend, the walking dead.

When I started first grade I was labeled a disruptive child in school by my teachers. I guess that was the label back then that they gave to kids who were hyperactive. Fortunately for me someone recognized what was going on with me and scheduled a meeting in school with my mother. During that meeting which I attended, they told my mother they wanted to give me a series of aptitude tests to determine my learning level. Whoever came up with this idea may have saved my life and didn't even know it. Lots of kids during that time were just punished and pumped full of drugs that made them sluggish and incoherent. I guess it was just the easiest thing to do back then.

After I took the aptitude tests my mother was called back into school for another meeting. What the school found out from the tests was that although I was in the first grade I was reading and doing schoolwork on a third-grade level. I attribute a lot of this to the fact that I loved to read and was curious about everything. Before I started school I could read and do math. My great grandmother was great. She constantly worked with me when I was small, teaching me things and reading to me. She had a dictionary, which I still have to this day, that I would constantly read and learn from. I also read old encyclopedias and magazines when I could get my hands on them.

I started out as a left hander, but when my great grandmother realized it she quickly made me start using my right hand to do things. Left-handed people were looked upon as odd back then. She wanted me to be right-handed because just about everything in life was set up for right-handed people. It sort of worked out because I ended up being ambidextrous.

When my mother returned to the school I remember the principal telling her that they needed to move me up to the third grade in order for me to be at my learning level. This would have put me with kids much older than me and made me look out of place. That's when they told my mother that there was a program that just started that would be ideal for me. They wanted to send me to a school in Litchfield County where their learning level was higher, and their first-grade learning level matched the learning level where I was. This program, however, required me to be bused there daily. This required me to take a forty-five-minute bus ride there and back every day. I don't know why my mother agreed to this, but I'm sure glad she did. Maybe she felt it kept me out of her hair longer every day.

For five years I took that ride and soaked up all the knowledge and cultural differences that came along with going to a rural school. It wasn't until I went to school there that I realized exactly how poor we were. When you're living around a bunch of people that are just like you everything seems normal because everyone is poor.

I did very well in school, but I carried a secret that haunted me for my entire life. My mother had never told me the identity of my biological father. From the time I was old enough to ask she always avoided the question. When I was around the kids in my neighborhood in Waterbury it was never an issue because most of the kids from my area came from broken homes with absentee fathers. It was more of the norm rather than the exception. My life growing up in my neighborhood was like a television game show called "Who's Your Daddy." This became even more obvious when I became an adult and started reading the obituaries. You would be surprised at who was whose father, sibling or relative when they died.

When I started attending school in Litchfield the family dynamics were very much different. Mostly all of the children in my classes came from traditional two parent, one family homes. This was very different than what I was accustomed to back in Waterbury and I started becoming ashamed of how I was living and being raised.

Shame had always made it difficult for me to talk about this subject and I didn't realize the effects it had on me throughout my life until now. I would avoid conversations about my family to everyone, not because they were mean or I was ashamed of them, but because I didn't think others from Litchfield would understand my situation. I didn't want to explain why my parents had a different last name than me or why I didn't look like my father. I never expressed this to my family in fear that they would take me out of this school and make me attend local public schools in Waterbury. I really liked the new environment and was willing to adapt to it. Once you are introduced to something better there is no turning back.

Around this time my mother met my future stepfather, Leroy. I say future because I don't know when they actually got married because my mother never told me. For all I know they were married when he moved in with us. For a while we all lived together in my great grandmother's apartment until they found an apartment to move into. I don't know if my mother left me behind with my great grandmother because she knew I wanted to stay there or if it was an easy way for her not to have to deal with me. Either way I'm glad I stayed.

I really enjoyed living with my great grandmother. Although you wouldn't think it to look at her, my great grandmother was sixty years old when I was born. We lived in a three-family home occupied with all family members. Me and my great grandmother were on the first floor, my grandmother and grandfather lived on the second floor and my uncle Fred lived on the third floor. Being the only child in the house I pretty much had full range of the entire building. Growing up around the older generation taught me a lot about our family history, at least on my mother's side of the family. I learned things about my ancestry that I would have never learned in school. It's amazing because now they want to ban books in school but not assault weapons. It just goes to show how frightened some people are of others learning the truth. They want their children and everyone else's to believe the same old racist, homophobic, antiquated beliefs that most of them grew up believing.

Although my great grandmother only had one child she raised several children in our family throughout the years. Before moving to Connecticut from South Carolina my great grandmother and great grandfather were the matriarch and patriarch of our family. Everyone called them mama and daddy because that's who they were to them.

To say my mother treated me badly would be an overstatement. She didn't treat me badly in a physical way, but she was never a loving type of mother. She didn't shower me with hugs and kisses and tell me how much she loved me. Till this day I can say my mother has never told me or said to me that she loves me. Maybe that's why some people say I don't smile and have an uninviting demeanor. Like I say, you can't make someone give you something they don't have.

I never had a birthday party or any kind of celebration growing up. Part of this was due to my grandmother being a Jehovah's Witness. When I did go on trips or family outings it wasn't because my mother arranged it, she just joined in with me and my grandparents.

I'm not faulting her; it was just who she was. My mother didn't grow up with her birth parents so to her it might have been normal for me not to have grown up with her. I know I wasn't the only kid who didn't grow up with their biological father, but it sure felt like I was. The sins of our parents are not our sins to carry but are sins we can learn from..

Revelation

November 2019 was the start of the Covid pandemic. This pandemic would eventually take the lives of millions of people all over the world. During the early part of the pandemic, I lost several family members due to its effects.

In March of 2020, my mother decided to go to the funeral of my stepfather's twin brother in South Carolina. I asked my mother not to go to the funeral due to the pandemic and the dangers it posed. Many people were wearing masks and the number of deaths from the pandemic was just starting to rise. One thing to know about my mother is that if she wants to do something there is no way of talking her out of it. When I told her it wasn't safe nor a good idea to travel during this time, especially not in a place where many people would be congregating, she said "Those news people don't know what they are talking about." There was no need in saying anymore to her.

Within the first week of my mother returning home from the funeral she became very ill from the virus. Her illness required her to be hospitalized for several weeks.

During this time most people who were hospitalized with the virus were usually dead within two weeks of their admission or they never returned home. During that time visitors weren't allowed to visit patients due to the risk of further infections from the virus. People who did want to visit their loved ones had to do so by video chat where the hospital had a monitor in a room so you could see your loved one as you spoke to them. I worried the entire time that my mother wasn't going to make it out. She had two things that didn't work in her favor. The first thing was that she was elderly, and the second thing was that she was African American. The virus seemed to have a harder impact on the African American population that it did on others. Those were the longest two weeks of my life waiting to see if my mother was going to make it. I don't take the death of close relatives and friends very well. Thankfully, my mother made a full recovery and was able to return home after a short stay in a rehabilitation center. Maybe God was sparing her for what was to come next.

As I got older my family history became more important to me. Unfortunately, I had to learn this the hard way. I constantly question myself as to why I never pursued the truth sooner. When I became an adult I should have asked my mother flat out, "who is my biological father and where is he today?" Deep down inside I wanted to, but something just kept stopping me from doing it. I guess because I thought I had gotten the truth from my great grandmother I figured there was no need in starting a fight with my mother over something that she made clear she didn't want to talk about. Besides, by this point I had already formed an opinion of my biological father as someone who didn't care about me so why should I care about him? The few times I did ask my mother about my biological father was when I was a child. She always pushed the narrative to me that he didn't do anything for me, and he didn't care about me. When you're a child that's a hard pill to swallow.

The bad part about exposing lies and finding new relatives that you never knew existed is that not everyone will be happy that you found them. Some will welcome you with open arms while others will push you away as if you were some kind stray animal looking for a warm home and a free meal. This can be both hurtful and disappointing, especially when you are just someone that wants to find their family.

I already knew this, so I came into this with an open mind. I made it clear to myself that whatever reaction I got from these family members I was willing to take, even if that meant rejection. I learned that from the time you are born the clock starts ticking and no one knows just how much time you have on it until it's gone. I would advise everyone if you have any unresolved issues to resolve them before your time is up or the answers that you are looking for disappear. The truth can be both hurtful and invigorating but the truth is always the truth. The truth is always better than the alternative.

My whole life changed in August of 2020 when a female approached my stepfather, Leroy, at his job with some unexpected news. This was not just any female; she was someone who me and my stepfather knew very well. Darlene was a local woman with a colorful past. Very loud and brash. The kind of person who spoke whatever was on her mind regardless of the fallout. Not the kind of person that would lie about anything. Her life was like an open book to everyone. When Darlene came into my stepfather's place of business she initially asked him if he had a number that she could contact me at.

Knowing how I am about my privacy, my stepfather told Darlene that she could give him her phone number and he would pass it along for me to contact her. He advised her that I probably wouldn't call if he didn't give me some information about what she wanted. Hesitant to say what it was about, Darlene just blurted it out to him, "I just found out that he's my brother." Leroy said he couldn't believe what he was hearing. Not only did my mother not tell me who my biological father was, she also never told him either. I couldn't imagine how someone could be married to a person for so many years and never tell them the truth about who their stepchild's biological father is. Leroy had been with me since I was a little boy and always treated me as his own.

Later that day when Leroy contacted me he said, "are you sitting down." When I answered yes he said a woman named Darlene had come to his office today and told him that she was my sister. I could hear the shock and surprise in his voice as I remained silent on the other end of the phone. Sensing that I didn't seem surprised by this news he asked, "did you know this?" My mother may not have told Leroy who my biological father was, but he knew who Darlene's father was.

As I took a deep breath I started to lay the story down to him. I told Leroy that I had been ready and waiting for this day for most of my life. I then told him the story of how my great grandmother had told me who she thought was my biological father and how I have been keeping this secret for more than fifty years. I told him that I vowed to myself that I would not go searching for anyone on my biological father's side of the family, but if I ever got approached by anyone I was going to want to know the whole truth. The reason it didn't shock me was because Darlene's father was the same man that my great grandmother had told me many years ago was my biological father.

Leroy was shocked beyond belief. He said that he knew Darlene's father very well and that he liked him. He said he was a very laid-back mellow guy. Leroy even seemed shocked to hear that David was my father because the term, dead beat dad, didn't fit his persona. I told Leroy that I had been expecting that someone one day might reach out to me, I just didn't expect it to be Darlene.

Still in shock, I told Leroy to give me the number and I would contact Darlene. I told him that once I get things figured out I would get back to him and let him know what was going on. I could tell that he too was relieved to finally learn the truth about my biological father, something that my mother had refused to even tell him. Leroy had been with me ever since I was a little boy and to me he was the only father that I knew. Leroy wished me good luck and said to me, "I'll talk to you later." I couldn't help but to think that he must have really loved my mother and me to stay with a woman who refused to tell him the truth about a son that he raised as his own.

As I discovered the truth about my family history I had no idea how many others would be involved or were suffering through similar experiences in life. Knowing this made it easier for me to talk about it. Now it was time to open that door that had been shut for so long. The door into the family I never knew.

Darlene

When it came time to call Darlene I was a little apprehensive, but I knew I had to make that call. This was the moment I had always been expecting but was never totally ready for. As I contemplated making the call, I sat for a moment starring at my cell phone screen saying to myself, "is this really happening?" A family secret I had been carrying for over fifty years was now going to be exposed. I knew that once I started snooping it wouldn't be long before my mother would find out and she would probably be furious. This woman valued her privacy like a treasure chest full of gold. She had no problem gossiping and talking about other people's business, but her business was off limits to everyone, including me. I didn't care though because I gave her ample time to address this with me and she never chose to do so. What she failed to realize is that her business was also my business. Me knowing how my mother operates, she never planned to talk about this and had planned on taking this one to the grave with her.

After what seemed like an hour I finally started dialing the digits on my phone. I knew this phone call was going to be the key to what would open up a whole new world to me. A world I knew existed, but never dared to enter. I was actually relieved. Deep down inside I always wanted to know the truth but never bothered to pursue it. Part of it was because I knew how my mother would react to it and the other part was because I felt as though I had been abandoned so why should I care about looking for someone who didn't want me? He knew where I was, why should I look for him, he's the one who abandoned me, right?

By this time Darlene's father, David, had been dead for two years. David died in November of 2018, the same year my mother slid his obituary over to me on the kitchen table and told me that he had passed away. Things were starting to add up now. I believe my mother knew all along that I thought David was my biological father. She probably figured someone had told me by now. I wouldn't be surprised if she didn't tell my great grandmother that David was my biological father because she knew my great grandmother would tell me eventually.

Somehow my mother had created this illusion to conceal the truth. I think she thought that by telling me David had died it would bring some closure to me without her ever having to say the words, "David was your father." I must admit she almost had me.

When I go back to that day in 2018 I remember saying to myself, "Why is she doing this?" It wasn't as if me and David had any relationship nor had my mother ever mentioned him to me. Maybe it was my police skills, but I knew something wasn't right with this. Things just weren't adding up.

After pushing the last number on my cell phone to call Darlene, I took a deep breath and waited for what was about to happen. When a woman answered I said, "May I speak to Darlene?" The woman then said in a calm voice that she was Darlene. That's when I told her who I was. What I wasn't prepared for was the story that she was about to tell me. Darlene said her mother, Francis, was starting to show signs of dementia and her mother told her that she had something to tell her. Darlene said one day when she was visiting her mother, her mother said that there was something she had to tell her about her father.

Darlene said her mother told her that David had another son and that she had another brother. Darlene had a brother on her mother's side and two other brothers on her father's side so she wondered who this could be.

Francis told Darlene that David had another son that neither she nor David ever told anyone about, and that son was a cop in town. Darlene said she couldn't believe what her mother was saying. At that moment Darlene said she had mixed feelings. She was happy to find out that she had another sibling, but mad that her mother and David had kept this secret from her all of these years. Francis not only told Darlene my name and who I was, but she also gave her detailed information about me as if she had been keeping tabs on me all these years. You would think that with all the interactions Darlene had with police over the years her mother would have told her this sooner. All I could think was maybe she didn't want Darlene confronting me that way, so she waited until I had retired from the police force and David was dead. Darlene said she cried after hearing this news but was also eager to find me. Little did Darlene know that I had a surprise for her.

After Darlene finished speaking, I told her that I already knew about David. I told Darlene that my great grandmother had told me about David when I was a young boy, but I didn't know that she was his daughter. I told Darlene that I made a promise to my great grandmother that I would not reveal to anyone that she had told me who my biological father was. That was a secret that I had kept up until this day. Darlene was blown away by this. Darlene told me that David had two girls by her mother and two boys with his wife, but he never said anything about another child. We continued to talk for a while, comparing information and taking notes before hanging up and promising to talk more about this later and possibly meeting up.

Just that quick my whole world had just been blown up. A secret I didn't think would ever be revealed, an unknown family and an untruthful mother. Stuff that soap operas are made of. I started having visions of me on one of those trashy talk shows spilling family secrets and throwing chairs at each other. Everyone is entitled to know the truth about their parents, right? This is something that should go without saying. Why was it so important to my mother to keep a secret that would eventually destroy her relationship with her oldest child? I will never understand her logic behind that. Sometimes I wonder if she understands her logic at times.

Throughout this journey Darlene and I stayed in touch to learn the truth about my family history and to figure out why my mother, her mother and David were keeping this secret. Unfortunately, Darlene passed away in 2024 due to complications from the injuries which had left her paralyzed for so many years. She may have had a colorful past, but I believe she had a pure heart. One thing she said to me before we did the DNA test was, "I don't care if the results say you're not my brother, in my heart you will always be my brother, and I want you to find the truth whatever it may be." That meant a lot to me. She wasn't a selfish person, and I believe she wanted the truth just as much as I did.

Darlene and I spoke on many occasions before her passing sharing information and life experiences. After hearing the struggles and abuse that she went through growing up it was no wonder that her life turned out the way it did. Quite frankly I'm surprised it didn't turn out worse. As a police officer I had seen my fair share of people who were down and out on their luck.

Society tells people to pull themselves up by their bootstraps when they had no boots in the first place. Throughout the years growing up I had seen Darlene in passing, but never got to know her. From what I had seen and heard about her she was a wild child. Me and her could have been no more the polar opposites. After she shared her upbringing with me it gave me a clearer picture of why she had become the person she was. I believe we are all victims of our environments, and our fates are sometimes decided for us by the littlest things.

Darlene said that as a young girl older men always seem to give her a lot of attention, attention that she desired. Darlene said she had that desire for attention because of her low self-esteem. This attention eventually lead to drug and alcohol abuse. From that point her life just spiraled out of control. Unable to get her life under control it continued like that until that dreadful day when she was shot sitting on her front porch. Darlene and another woman were sitting on her porch at about one a.m. in the morning when a flurry of bullets meant for a local drug dealer rang out. When the dust had cleared Darlene said that she and the other woman had been hit.

Darlene's injuries were devastating, and she would never walk again. Darlene told me that since she's been in this wheelchair she has had time to reflect on her life. It was like a movie that continued to play over and over again. Many times, over the years, as if it were on a reel. For someone who had been through so much she still had the will and desire to go on even through her darkest days.

I don't believe in coincidences. I believe everything happens for a reason even if I don't know what that reason is. Darlene was brought into my life for a reason, and I won't stop until I find out what that reason was for. I believe it was for me to finally learn the truth about my family history. I owe that much to me and her to finish this search.

This new revelation led to that day in August of 2020 when my mother would put on full display to me exactly what kind of person she truly was. That's when I truly opened my eyes and mind to accept who she really was.

August 2020

On a sunny day in August of 2020, I finally had to confront my mother about this new revelation. It wasn't my plan to confront her that day, but she left me no choice in the matter. I wanted to have all my facts together before I confronted my mother and allow her the opportunity to tell me her side of the story. Right now, all I had was speculations, theories, and rumors.

Sometimes we have no say over when and where things happen in our lives, and we just have to go with the flow. I remember entering my mother's home that day as I normally did on Sundays for dinner, but before I could fix a plate of food and sit down she confronted me about Darlene. I had no intentions on telling my mother about Darlene until after I had all my facts straight, but I guess those plans were now all blown up now.

My mother started out with her typical loud voice and angry looks as she said to me, "did you get that girl and those lies straightened out?" That right there told me that my stepfather had said something to her. My stepfather could be well intentioned but could also have a big mouth. Knowing him it was just a chance to throw a dig to my mother for all her years of secrecy. After hearing that I knew this conversation was not going to go well.

I knew Darlene wasn't lying about what she had told me, but I didn't have the proof to confirm it. She was only telling me what she and her mother believed to be the truth, so I just let my mother continue to rant until there was a break in her yelling. I knew with time I would find the answers that I was looking for. When she seemed to pause for a second I knew this was the time to say it. At that point I couldn't hold it in anymore. I started out calm by telling her that Darlene wasn't lying and that maybe she should finally tell me the truth of who my biological father is. My mother then went on to belittle Darlene, talking about her promiscuous ways and criminal past as if that had anything to do with who my biological father was. This was nothing more than my mother deflecting from the question.

I stood quietly as my mother's voice continued to rise, her facial expressions showing her anger at having to talk about an issue she had hoped would never come up. She then went on to insinuate that Darlene was just trying to use me for whatever she could get out of me as if I were someone who was easily manipulated. Maybe my mother thought this because she had manipulated me for so many years. When it finally got to the point where I had enough I told my mother, "Ok, let's end this right here, right now. Who is my biological father?"

Those must have been the magic words as the room suddenly became as quiet as an empty church. My mother the angry, loud Black woman shut up and shut down instantly. The angry look disappeared from her face, like the sun going down over the horizon at the end of the day and her voice returned to a normal tone as if we had not been in a heated discussion earlier. Imagine the audacity of me to demand to know who my biological father is. This must have come as a surprise to her because I'm usually laid back and easy going, but not this time. I wanted an answer, and I wanted it now! I had been patient with my mother for way too long and now my patience had run out.

As I waited for her answer I could see she was struggling to find one, so I said it again, "Who is my biological father and where is he?'

I could tell the sense of panic that came over her. She's used to controlling a conversation but this time she had been out matched. As I pushed for an answer she blurted one out without thinking. Not wanting to tell the truth she blurted out the first lie that came to her mind, "I don't know."

Now I know my mother and I know when she is lying. My mother had never been some promiscuous woman with a laundry list of men. She never drank, smoked, or cursed. For what it's worth no one even knew of my mother seeing any man so to believe that she all of a sudden decided to have sex with some random stranger was highly unlikely. Out of respect I said to her, "Do you really want to tell your adult son that you have no idea who his biological father is?" I could tell she was scared because the moment she never thought would happen just attacked her like a rabid cat on a mouse. My mother may have been a lot of things but sleeping around in the streets wasn't one of them.

After a brief pause she said, "I think his name was Bubba or Bill." I then said to her "do you have a last name and where he is now?" I knew I had her on the ropes, so I wasn't going to let up. She said the last she knew he was from North Carolina or out in California. My mother never gave me his last name or an exact location for him, but she gave me enough to know that she knew more than she was letting on. The way my mother thinks is that by not saying anything means she isn't lying, but as far as I'm concerned concealing the truth when you're being asked a question directly is the same as lying.

My mother was good at concealing the truth but terrible at hiding it from me. After a brief pause I told my mother that I could find the truth, but don't make me have to do it the hard way. I was a police officer so finding the truth is something I did on a regular. I told her if I have to find out what I'm looking for the hard way this will probably be the last time we ever speak. You would think hearing something like that from your son would tell you just how serious he was, but not my mother. Concealing her lie was more important to her than telling the truth. She should have chosen her next words more wisely.

She then proceeded to tell me that I better not tell my siblings about this because they will be mad at me. Now this made no sense to me. Why would my siblings be mad at me for asking her who my biological father was? I had the right to know, right? But I knew exactly what she meant. My mother was good at creating resentment amongst her children. She had been doing this as long as I can remember. I knew that meant she was going to give them some alternate truth of what had taken place today and frame herself as the victim to them.

My sister and mother have always had an on again, off again relationship so I knew she wouldn't buy whatever my mother was going to try and sell her, but my brother is a momma's boy. He would just soak up whatever she said and accept it as the truth. All it would be for him is just another excuse to hate me. The audacity of my mother to treat me as though I wronged her. The nerve of her to even suggest distorting the truth to make herself look like the victim. Because of this my relationship with my siblings was forever changed due to my mother's lying.

Now some may say this was harsh of me to walk out on my mother like that and never speak to her again, but that's because they don't know the whole story. It's easy for one to judge a situation when they aren't the one going through it.

If you speak to a lot of people they will give you an image of my mother as a nice young woman from the south, but that's not the person she was to me.

This day had been coming for a long time. It was easy to ignore my mother's devious ways when my great grandmother and grandmother were alive because they always showed me love and affection. I always had them to go to, so I just tuned my mother out. But when they died all I had was my mother left. Make no mistake, I didn't just levitate to my mother, some close friends coerced me to spend more time with my mother while she was alive. I don't know if that was the right thing to do but I made the attempt anyway. Society tries to make you believe that you automatically owe your parents some kind of love, respect, and attention, but you don't. Your parents may have brought you into this world, but they also carry the responsibility of being loving, caring, and maintaining your respect for them.

Never go against your better judgement. As I later learned from my newfound siblings they too had similar stories of growing up with their parents and how they struggled with their dilemmas.

When my great grandmother and grandmother were alive I would sometimes go months without seeing or speaking to my mother. It wasn't like she lived out of state or across the country. Most of the time growing up she lived in the same neighborhood as me. Obviously, it didn't bother her either because she made no attempt to check in with me either. I know she had two other children living with her, but do you just forget about the other one just because he doesn't live with you? I was aware of this too because I remember one time as a kid saying to myself, "I haven't seen or talked to my mother in over nine months." I didn't know what it was like to be raised by my mother, but if my sister and brother's behaviors is any indication it probably wasn't good. Before all of this broke out my sister would say horrible things about my mother to me that I didn't want to believe. Now I wonder if there was any truth to some of it.

It's now 2024 and I haven't spoken to my mother since that day in 2020. I don't hate my mother, I just dislike some of her ways. I haven't spoken to her out of respect. The way she has treated me throughout this ordeal and her continuous lying has made me lose respect for her. It's very difficult for me to talk to someone that I have lost respect for and then be respectful to them all at the same time. After all she is still my mother, and I can respect that. I did, however, write her a letter in 2021 laying out my feelings and what I found out about my history. I even said in the letter to my mother that my father had died at the age of fifty-two and he had lupus. There could be things I needed to know about him for medical purposes. I told her that she could contact me anytime if she wanted to. Unfortunately, that day has never come, and I don't think it ever will. I don't know if she is more upset that I found out the truth about her dark secret or that Darlene was the one to expose it. Either way it doesn't excuse her behavior.

What I wasn't totally prepared for was my mother's actions over the next few years as I tried to unravel this web of lies. I expected her to be mad, but she went scorched earth on me. She bad mouthed me to whoever would listen, she started referring to me as "that boy" to family members and even refused to let me get my family photos which I had left at her home before this incident occurred. I knew my mother had a temper and anger issues but now it was on full display for me and everyone else to see.

I gave my mother the opportunity to make this right on so many occasions, but she consistently failed to rise to the occasion. I know the older someone gets the harder it is for them to change, but change is possible, you just have to want it bad enough and I guess my mother didn't.

There's not a day that goes by when I don't think of that dreadful day. My mother's look, her dreadful tone, and her habitual lying. I will never be able to understand why lying to everyone, especially during this stage in her life, was so important to her. I knew going forward was going to force me to drudge up old, suppressed memories. Things I hadn't forgotten but rather chose to not think or talk about, but I had to do this if I was ever going to find out who I truly was and tell my story.

My mother's refusal to tell the truth also started another rumor. This rumor was that maybe my step grandfather might be my biological father. I loved my step grandfather very much and he was one of the most honorable men I ever knew. Just the thought of anyone thinking that he could do such a thing made my skin crawl.

I knew my next step was necessary to not only clear David's name, but to also squash any ridiculous rumors about my step grandfather being my father.

DNA

Within a week of our initial conversation, I contacted Darlene again. She told me that she had told her sister about me as well as David's two other sons. Darlene said that David's oldest son was skeptical about this and said that he didn't believe his father would do such a thing, and quite frankly I didn't either. I had my doubts from the beginning. I knew my great grandmother wouldn't lie to me, but something just didn't seem right about this.

I told Darlene this is the type of situation I was hoping I would never be in. David seemed like a really nice guy, and I didn't want anyone smearing his name just to protect their secret. By now the speculation that my step grandfather was my father had started to gain some traction. I didn't want any ridiculous rumors spreading about my step grandfather being my biological father either. Both of these men deserved better than that. My step grandfather died when I was fourteen years old. I remember it like it was yesterday because we were planning on going to the

Bradley Air Museum the next day. I was on the third floor at the time listening to some albums in my uncle's apartment when I heard my grandmother scream. I'll never forget the album that I was playing when this happened. It was the group, A Taste of Honey. I quickly ran downstairs and saw my step grandfather slumped over in his chair where he watched the television in the den every day. I could tell by his labored breathing that he was in cardiac arrest. I had learned CPR in school in Litchfield, so I was familiar with what to do in these situations. When I saw my step grandfather take his last breathe I quickly put him on the floor and started performing CPR on him until the ambulance arrived. The paramedics took over when they arrived but quickly stopped their efforts when there was no sign of life. As they covered him up to take him away I remember one of the paramedics asking me how I knew what to do. I told him I learned CPR in school. He then said you're a brave kid. You did everything you could but there was no bringing him back at that point. They believe he had a massive heart attack. That day would forever be burned into my memory. It wasn't until after the funeral that my mind was able to fully process that he was gone forever.

I told Darlene I think the best thing for us to do is to take a DNA test to remove any doubt and to clear David and my step grandfather's name. Although I didn't know David personally I sensed that he was a good man that didn't deserve this rumor if it was a lie. Besides both men were dead and unable to defend for themselves so I knew I needed to do it for them. Fortunately for me Darlene agreed to the DNA test. I could tell she was just as eager as I was to know the truth.

Darlene shared with me during our conversations her dislike of David. She said she didn't care if she found out he wasn't her father. Darlene felt that when David married a younger woman and started a family he just forgot about her and her sister. Darlene said he was a great provider and would give them whatever they needed or asked for, but he didn't spend much time with them. Darlene believed it was his new wife that didn't want his daughters around and kept David at a distance. Darlene just felt that he could have done a better job as a father.

The following week I received in the mail the DNA test kit that I had ordered. I then contacted Darlene and told her about it and then we set up a date for me to go to her home to get her DNA test sample. I was relieved and scared all at the same time.

Either I was going to exonerate a man or have to confront the possible reality of a terrible rumor. What if David wasn't my father, then what? Where do I go from there? Could my step grandfather be my biological father? My feelings were mixed, but I was positive that I had to go through with this. Finding the truth would take a heavy load off my shoulders and possibly clear a man's name. David nor my step grandfather didn't deserve to have their names dragged through the mud if they were innocent parties in this drama.

When I arrived at Darlene's home she was there with her stepdaughter. Her stepdaughter was a big help in assisting Darlene in her everyday needs. Darlene was paralyzed from the waist down, the result of a stray bullet striking her in the back as an innocent civilian many years ago. Her stepdaughter was very nice and helpful in assisting Darlene with taking the test sample. Her stepdaughter even shared with me her personal story of not finding out who her biological father was until he approached her on the street when she was sixteen years old.

She said as far as she knew the man who raised her was her biological father. She didn't know if the man who raised her ever knew that she wasn't his biological daughter because he passed away before the truth came out. Just like me she said her relationship with her mother was over when the truth was finally exposed. Although she said her relationship with her mother was over when she found out who her biological father was, I know from experience that there were probably other long-term issues between her and her mother just as there were with mine.

We continued to talk for a few before we did the DNA test sample. Just hearing someone else's story helped erase some of the shame and hurt that I carried for so many years of not knowing who my biological father was. I said to myself, here is someone that totally understands what I'm going through.

After getting Darlene's DNA test sample I told them that I would be mailing them out today and should have an answer within the next few weeks. When the DNA test results were returned that would explain my mother's anger and denials. It was a strange feeling at first doing the DNA. On one hand I wanted it to come back positive for David being my father just to end the speculation, but on the other hand I wanted the truth no matter what it was. I couldn't wait to put an end to all the mystery surrounding the identity of my biological father. After getting the DNA test results back it explained why my mother wasn't concerned about me finding out that David wasn't my father, she was concerned about what else I would find out.

When I was in my early twenties I made a bet with a friend that taught me a very valuable lesson in life. My friend had a motorcycle, and he said the engine on it had points for an ignition system in it. Now I worked on motorcycles, and I knew for a fact that there were no points installed in motorcycle engines that year. He said to me if you're so sure then let's make a bet. He said to me twenty dollars says there are points in this motor. I was eager to make that bet because I knew I was a sure winner, or at least I thought I was. After making the bet he removed the ignition cover and what did I see, a points ignition. I lost the bet! I couldn't believe it. He laughed and said keep your money I just wanted to teach you a lesson. He said he had the upper hand on me because he knew for sure what was under the cover because he had changed them, but me on the other hand was basing my bet on my knowledge of those motors, not from what I knew for a fact about this motor. He told me to never bet against someone who has the upper hand on you. They know what they know, you on the other hand are just speculating. It was a lesson I remembered and applied throughout my life. That was the reason why I didn't think David was my father, my mother was too confident that he wasn't.

Although Darlene was confined to a wheelchair it amazed me at how tall she stood when she believed in something. Here was a woman who had been shot in the back as an innocent bystander and paralyzed for life, but now put all of that to the side to help me learn the true identity of my biological father. She didn't do it because she had to, she did it because she wanted to. I could tell that she wanted me to be happy and find the truth.

As we waited for the DNA test results a lot of things ran through my head. All those years that I use to see this woman and just brushed her off as one of those women who just lost her way, not knowing that maybe she didn't lose her way, maybe she was pushed that way. I believe as people we are all broken and or damaged to a certain degree, but we all have a reset button. You just have to know when to take the initiative and push it. Everyone deserves a second chance in life. I really hope that Darlene gets hers. I couldn't think of anyone else at this time who deserved it more than her.

The DNA Results

After several weeks of waiting for the DNA test results they arrived. The moment of truth was finally here. I sat for a minute to gather my thoughts before opening the letter. The day I had been waiting for was finally upon me and I was going to get my answers. I knew opening that letter was either going to solve some curiosities or open up a whole new batch of worms.

As I slowly opened the envelope and removed the letter it revealed what I had feared and what my mother knew, Darlene and I were not a match. Actually, we shared nothing in common. Now the question was, "Is David not my father?" "Is David Darlene's father?" "Is David either of our father?" This DNA test result has now opened up more questions than answers. I knew Darlene would be disappointed with these results because she had become fond of me by this time. Before I broke this news to Darlene I had to go over every possible scenario first.

I didn't want to disappoint her with inaccurate information. That's when it dawned on me, David has a living sister. The next day I contacted Darlene and told her about the DNA test results. She was calm as she said, "well, maybe he isn't my father." Darlene didn't care because she didn't care for David anyway. I then told Darlene that there was another way. If David's sister agrees to do the DNA test then we would know for sure if he was either of our fathers. I told Darlene that I would contact David's sister and see if she would be willing to do a DNA test.

Later that day I stopped by David's sister, Julia, home. Julia was no stranger to me because I grew up next door to her and her son, Bernard. Me and her son use to play together in our backyards. I liked Julia and she was always very friendly to me. After greeting her I had to tell her the reason for why I was there. It had been many years since I had seen Julia so this would seem odd that I just showed up. When I explained the controversy of David possibly being my father she was shocked. Her exact words were, "If David had a child and didn't tell me I will go to that grave and dig him up."

Julia was not happy at all. I told Julia that a sample of her DNA could clear this all up and determine if David was my father or not.

Julia was agreeable but concerned about my mother being angry if she found out that she had helped me. I told Julia that I wouldn't tell her how I got the information and that I just wanted to finally know the truth. When she agreed I told her that I would order the DNA test kit and return with it to get her sample. Maybe now I could finally put this issue to rest.

The question swirling around in my head now was, what if she is no relation to me? I figured I'd cross that bridge when I got to it. This was already more than my mind could take at this moment and the truth was more important than any possible disappointment. Fate so had it that this would be the last time I spoke to Julia. A darker truth was just around the corner, ready to rear its ugly head.

Although I did the DNA test to find out the identity of my biological father, it also opened up other secrets that my mother had kept from me like the identity of her father, my biological grandfather. Growing up I always assumed my grandmother's husband was my mother and uncle's father. It wasn't until after my step grandfather died that it became known to me that my mother and uncle had two different fathers. I didn't even know until now that my mother's real surname was Green, not Abney. I found this out from my stepfather and their marriage certificate. My mother was born Sallie Mae Green. She adopted the Abney surname because she and her brother grew up together with my great grandmother and great grandfather who had the Abney surname. She never officially changed her name to Abney; she just used it.

The deeper I got into my family history the more dysfunctional it was sounding to me. I was so ashamed of not knowing who my biological father was that it never dawned on me that I didn't know who my biological grandfather was either. At this point I wasn't even sure if I knew who my mother was. Now not only did I need to find out who was on my father's side of the family, I also needed to explore my mother's father's side of the family. I knew I was going to have my work cut out for me.

I have always been the type of person that took control of things in my life that I had control of, but there was only so much control I had over this situation. I would just keep searching and let the cards fall where they may.

Tiffany

The last few months have been tumultuous for me to say the least. I was doing everything that I had vowed I would never do. I was upending people's lives, exposing things that some people never wanted exposed and doing DNA testing, but I guess you got to crack a few eggs in order to make an omelet.

When me and Darlene found out that we weren't a DNA match I did something I didn't want to do, I made my DNA profile public. You have to be careful with that because you have no idea what kind of can of worms you could be opening. But, by this point my curiosity and anger were so high that I was willing to do whatever it took to get to the truth. I was so focused on learning the identity of my biological father that I never even thought that this would also expose the identity of my mother's father whom I never knew. I was about to kill two birds with one stone.

Upon going online and logging into the Ancestry website to order another DNA test kit, the message tab was lit.

When I clicked on it there was a message from a woman who was unknown to me. Upon reading the message the woman identified herself as Tiffany and she said that according to the DNA matches she was my sister. I had to calm myself for a moment because I thought this was some kind of joke. This woman was from California. I don't even know anyone in California. I had to take a moment to let this process before responding.

Because I was so emotional at this time it had totally slipped my mind that my mother had mentioned that my biological father was either in North Carolina or California as far as she knew. I knew I couldn't go back and speak to my mother about this because that door had been closed. After I finished reading the message I decided to check my DNA matches. Low and behold there she was, Tiffany, a perfect DNA match as my sibling. Still not convinced I responded back to her. If she were my sister how could this be? I proceeded to ask Tiffany, who are your parents? Tiffany said she was biracial, her mother is White, but her father was Black. His name was William Lee Felton and he had originated from

Connecticut. My next obvious question was, "when did he leave Connecticut?" She said he came to California in 1966, two years after I was born. Now she had my attention. Tiffany said her mother was much younger than William when she meet him at the Zodiac Motorcycle Club. William was a member of the club and portrayed himself to be younger than he actually was. Tiffany said she didn't go to his funeral, but he passed away in 1994 and that he had two other sons in California. My mind was racing because if what she was saying is true that meant my mother deliberately kept this from me in order to cover up her lies. Here I am thinking my father died in 2018 when he actually died in 1994. I was beyond upset at this point. I asked Tiffany if we could speak over the phone, and she said yes.

Tiffany quickly messaged me her cell phone number and I proceeded to call her. Tiffany and I had a good conversation as we tried to sort through this mystery. Tiffany then sent me the only picture she had of her and our father. She was about a year old in that picture that was taken shortly before her mother and father split up. She stated that her parents broke up about a year after she was born, and she never had any contact with her father because her mother had a restraining order out against him. According to Tiffany she said her mother told her that our father was abusive. One day her mother told her that she came home and found a mark on her leg where our father had hit her because she was crying. That was her breaking point. She took Tiffany and left William and never looked back. She even got a restraining order to prevent him from going anywhere near them.

When I told Tiffany that I was a retired police officer she said cool. Tiffany told me that she had four children, one from a previous marriage. She said her present husband is a Sheriff Department Deputy in Los Angeles and that she too had wanted to become an officer but abandoned the idea after starting her family.

At that point Tiffany told me that I should speak to our brother Darryl because he knew our father best. Tiffany gave me Darryl's contact information and I told her that I would stay in touch. I was beginning to feel as if this were going to turn into something bigger than

I could have ever imagined, but there was no stopping me at this point. The most remarkable thing I found out later was although we were siblings we all had very different upbringings and stories to share. As I gradually tracked down and spoke to each of my siblings, they shared their experiences growing up and helped me to better understand how we all got to this point. To better understand what was going on I had to break down each sibling's story.

Growing Up

It's easy to see a finished product and think the road to completion was easy, but for me and my siblings we all carried a label or labels as we grew up with in this country.

First we were all Black children which meant we faced different challenges in America than others from different ethnicities. Second we were all children from broken families which are often defined as those that come from divorced, separated, or single parents. Third we all came from poor to middle class households, which limited our choices in life. In our case we checked all three boxes. This can lead to impact emotional, social, and psychological development, but somehow we all seemed to make it. As I tell each story you will see how we fit into the various categories of children from broken homes.

Children from broken homes may experience a deep sense of loss when their parents separate, which can lead to feelings of sadness, grief, or abandonment. The absence of one parent or the upheaval in family dynamics can create a sense of insecurity. Children may worry about the stability of their living situation, financial security, or future relationships. Children might feel torn between their parents, especially if there is conflict or tension between them. They may feel pressured to choose sides or worry about disappointing one parent.

The emotional stress from family disruptions can affect a child's concentration and motivation, potentially leading to lower academic achievement. Some children may exhibit behavioral issues such as aggression, defiance, or withdrawal. These behaviors can be a response to the stress and confusion they feel about their family situation.

Studies have shown that children from broken families may be at a higher risk of experimenting with drugs or alcohol as a coping mechanism.

Children from broken families may struggle to form or maintain friendships due to trust issues or fear of rejection. They might also have a harder time forming healthy romantic relationships later in life. Children from broken homes may also feel different from their peers, especially if their family situation is less common in their social circle. This can lead to feelings of isolation or being misunderstood.

The instability and stress of living in a broken family can increase the risk of anxiety and depression in children. They may struggle with feelings of worthlessness or guilt, believing they are somehow responsible for the family breakdown. The absence of a parent, especially in cases where there is minimal contact, can lead to low self-esteem. Children might internalize the separation and believe they are not worthy of love or attention.

Single-parent households often face financial difficulties, which can limit access to resources like quality education, extracurricular activities, or even basic needs. This can create additional stress for the child. Financial constraints may also limit opportunities for the child, such as traveling, participating in sports, or attending special programs, which can affect their social development and self-confidence.

Children from broken families might have a more pessimistic view of relationships and marriage, leading to difficulties in forming long-term commitments. However, not all outcomes are negative; some children develop strong resilience, independence, and critical thinking skills as they navigate their family situation. Support from extended family, friends, or counselors can play a crucial role in fostering these positive outcomes.

This was just the beginning of our struggles. We also grew up during the aids and crack cocaine epidemics which surged throughout the 1980's and into the early 1990's. Being from the inner cities we were more likely to be affected by these epidemics more than others who weren't from our areas.

These epidemics were extremely detrimental to African Americans who most frequented these areas. The crack cocaine epidemic of the 1980s and 1990s was a major public health and social crisis in the United States that had devastating effects on many urban communities.

Cocaine use in the U.S. surged in the late 1970s and early 1980s, particularly among wealthier populations. However, the high cost of powdered cocaine made it inaccessible to many lower-income individuals.

Crack cocaine was a cheaper, smokable form of cocaine making it more popular amongst those who were unable to afford the higher price of regular cocaine. It quickly spread in urban areas, particularly in poor communities. Those communities that me and my siblings grew up in.

Crack cocaine was cheap and had a highly addictive nature which led to widespread use. I saw many people whom I grew up with become addicted to it and ruin their lives. Many even died from it. The crack epidemic disproportionately affected African American communities, contributing to racial disparities in health, crime, and incarceration rates.

The AIDS epidemic, which began in the early 1980s, had a profound and disproportionate impact on the African American community in the United States. These are some of the impacts that it had on us:

The emergence of HIV/AIDS. The first cases of what would be later known as AIDS (acquired immunodeficiency syndrome) were reported in the United States in 1981. It was soon linked to (HIV) Human Immunodeficiency Virus which attacks the body's immune system, leaving individuals vulnerable to opportunistic infections and certain cancers. Initially the epidemic was most visible among gay men, but it quickly spread to other populations including intravenous drug users, hemophiliacs, and heterosexual individuals.

Early in the epidemic there was a significant stigma and fear surround HIV/AIDS, partly due to its association with marginalized communities such as gay men and drug users. This stigma often led to discrimination and delayed efforts to address the crisis effectively.

Although African Americans represent a smaller percentage of the U.S. population, they have consistently accounted for a higher proportion of new HIV infections and AIDS diagnoses. Several factors contributed to the disproportionate impact on African Americans, including higher rates of poverty, limited access to healthcare, and the prevalence of other sexually transmitted infections (STIs) that increase the risk of HIV transmission.

The broader societal stigma surrounding HIV/AIDS was compounded by racism, resulting in discriminatory practices in healthcare, employment, and housing for African Americans with HIV/AIDS. African American women have been particularly hard-hit by the epidemic, often contracting HIV through heterosexual contact. They have represented a significant proportion of new infections among women in the U.S.

Young African Americans, especially gay and bisexual men, have faced high rates of HIV infection, influenced by factors such as lack of comprehensive sex education, homophobia, and limited access to preventive services like condoms and pre-exposure prophylaxis (PrEP).

The introduction of Highly Active Antiretroviral Therapy (HAART) in the mid-1990s transformed HIV/AIDS from a fatal disease to a manageable chronic condition for those with access to treatment. However, disparities in access to these life-saving medications meant that African Americans were less likely to benefit from these advances.

African Americans continue to face higher rates of new HIV infections and are less likely to receive timely treatment compared to other racial and ethnic groups. Addressing these disparities requires ongoing efforts to improve healthcare access, reduce stigma, and tackle the root causes of inequality.

As you can see, me and my siblings survived a lot to make it to where we are today. It must have been destiny for us to survive and eventually unite. Maybe one day we will all be able to get together for a family reunion to meet.

Darryl

After talking to Tiffany, I waited a day before I contacted Darryl. I guess you could say I was a little apprehensive seeing this whole experience was so new to me. How do you start off a conversation with a brother you never knew you had? We were complete strangers yet also siblings. I wasn't sure how he would take to this new revelation. Would he be mad? Would he reject the notion that I was his brother? I didn't know which direction this conversation was going to go but I knew I had to have it. After a short procrastination period, I built up the courage to make the call to Darryl.

When Darryl answered the phone his voice was warm and friendly, which helped to ease some of my anxieties. Our conversation flowed as if we had known each other our entire lives. Although we shared the same father, it was weird hearing Darryl refer to him as pops. I felt obligated to explain to Darryl how these revelations all came about, after all up until this week he had no idea I even existed. The more we talked the more things began to make sense.

Darryl even told me that he was born in Waterbury, Connecticut but his parents move to California when he was just a year old. Dates, times, and whereabouts were all in order. It was now becoming evident to me that my mother probably didn't want anyone to know about William because she was ashamed.

William was married to another woman, Cheryl, when my mother became pregnant by him. Cheryl was the mother of three of my siblings, Kim, Tracey, and Diane, but we will get into their lives later. I believe that maybe this was the reason for all the secrecy, but knowing my mother she didn't need a reason, if she didn't want to tell you something she just wouldn't tell you. As Darryl and I spoke he shared with me that he had two children from a previous marriage and that he is in another marriage now. He has a daughter that lives in Texas and a son that recently moved to Las Vegas. The more Darryl spoke the more information he shared with me. I now started to paint a picture in my mind of the timeline of some of the events.

By 1965 our father had three sons, one daughter, a pregnant wife, and a failing marriage. During this time William decided to separate from his wife leaving her to fend for herself with two small children and one on the way. In December of 1965 William and Cheryl's divorce was finalized and he was now free to be with Darryl's mother, Dixie. This left Cheryl distraught and with an uncertain future. Cheryl would go on to have their third child, a baby girl named Dianne. Cheryl lead William and everyone else to believe that the baby had died in the hospital at birth, but she didn't. She left the baby at the hospital for adoption. That child later reappeared as Diane.

Darryl stated that when his parents moved to California the reason our father gave them for the move was because of his asthma. I'm no scientist but I never heard of anyone moving to Los Angeles for better air quality. I believe William's decision to move his family to California was for more personal reasons.

In August of 1967, our brother David was born. Judging by the time of the move it appeared that Dixie was pregnant in Waterbury, Connecticut with David before moving to California. One year after the birth of David our father enlisted into the US Army where he served one year in active duty.

He was deployed overseas in December of 1968 to Vietnam where he served six months. Our father seemed to have a way with women which leaves the speculation of there being more siblings overseas or elsewhere. But for now, we are just going to stick to what we know.

Darryl enlisted in the ROTC when he was in high school and participated in it for a few years. When it came time for graduation Darryl stated that he attempted to enter the military but was turned down because he was unable to pass the comprehension part of the entry process.

As Darryl began to share his life and upbringing with me, he told me about four more siblings we had in California and Connecticut. He said we had a deceased sister named Kim and a brother named Tracey, both born to the same mother, Cheryl, in Waterbury, Connecticut and two sisters, Ave and Keisha that were both born in California to two different mothers.

Diane wasn't mentioned because Darryl didn't know she existed until I found out about her later on through Tracey.

In the course of a week, I had learned about a father and seven new siblings that I never knew existed before. I don't know why but finding out I had a deceased sister kind of hit me differently. I guess knowing that I would never get the chance to meet her just made me sad.

Darryl said that his mother was mean towards him growing up but not to our brother David. Maybe it was his closeness to our father and his resemblance of him that made Dixie act that way with him. Darryl said that the opposite was true of David. David didn't get along with our father and their mother treated David differently than she treated him.

There was something else though. I was familiar with Tracey. I didn't know him personally, but he traveled in some of the same circles as I when I was young man. Here I was walking right past my brother and never even knew it. Parents have no idea how bad keeping these secrets and lying to cover them up can destroy their children's and others' lives. One can only imagine how many relationships there are out there between relatives that never knew they were related. The psychological and physical effects could destroy them.

After Darryl told me their ages and dates of birth I was able to start a timeline of events. Based on the information I had obtained, Kim was born in Waterbury, Connecticut in April of 1963. In February of 1964 I was born in Waterbury, Connecticut. In March of 1965 Tracey was born and Darryl was born in September of 1965, both in Waterbury, Connecticut. David was born in August of 1967 in Los Angeles, California and Diane was born in February of 1966 in Waterbury, Connecticut, but I will get into that story later. Talk about a tight grouping. According to Darryl his mother and Tracey's mother were pregnant at the same time in 1965. I believe that the discovery of Darryl's mother's pregnancy is what eventually led to William and Cheryl getting divorced. By December of 1965 William and Cheryl's divorce had been finalized.

To say I was blown away by all of this would be an understatement, but I was glad to finally get some answers to questions that have been haunting me for decades. Darryl was my biggest window into the world of a father and siblings that I never knew. The good, the bad and everything in between. I was very fortunate to have a brother like him. Darryl also shared with me some of his health background. He recently had a mild stroke amongst other health issues with which he was dealing with. I knew that after talking to Darryl that a trip to California would be in my near future. I also now knew I had to track down the other siblings if I was going to complete this puzzle. My goal now was to at least locate and contact each sibling, so we all knew about each other, and no one was left in the dark. Hearing Darryl speak of our father and his experience growing up with him really made William seem like an average guy. The stories and pictures of them growing up was like watching a silent movie of them in slow motion.

Next on my list to contact would be David. Darryl had his contact information so he should be easy to reach, or at least I thought. Darryl had already warned me about what to expect from David if I did reach him. According to

Darryl, David was a member of a street gang and had been in and out of prison for most of his life. Darryl said he sometimes goes through periods of time of not even hearing from him and then out of the blue he will show up. I figured I came this far so I wasn't going to change my goal of locating and speaking to all of my siblings now.

David

Contacting David was turning out to be more difficult than I had expected. I tried reaching him by phone several times with no response. I even left messages that went unreturned. I was already warned by Darryl about the lifestyle our brother lived so there were no surprises to me. David has been involved in street gangs since he was a teenager and even spent many years in prison so the last person he probably wanted to hear from was a brother who was a retired cop. Like they say once you're in a gang, you're always in a gang.

According to Darryl, David and our father had a tumultuous relationship. Darryl said that after our father had come back from the military he always spoke to them as if they were soldiers in the military. He never ask them to do anything, he ordered them to do it. Darryl also said that our father told him that he questioned whether or not David was even his biological son. I don't know if there were any trust issues going on with him and Dixie or if it was the fact that David didn't want to listen to him. Either way they just didn't get along.

I would later find out that David was indeed William's son through DNA tests. David's son Davon had also taken a DNA test, and he came back as a match for me, being my nephew.

Growing up as a little brother for some people is hard. They're always trying to live up to or trying to outdo the older brother. Maybe that's what drove David to the street gang life. Darryl said over the years our father always encouraged him to stay away from David because of his gang activities. Maybe David wanted a family that accepted him for who he was. David's decision not to answer his phone or call me didn't deter me. I was determined to at least speak to him once and let him decide what type of relationship he did or did not want to have with me. Sometimes people need more time to process things. This was a lot for anyone to have to take in all at once.

At this time, it didn't seem as though I was going to be able to reach David, but I wasn't writing him off yet. I knew he was aware that I was his older brother because Darryl told me he had told him. This was a lot to take in for anyone, so I felt best to leave him his space.

It was interesting hearing Darryl speak of their upbringing with our father. Our father was obviously a complicated man just like so many men were during that time period. Growing up in a neighborhood with so many fathers like that gave me a lot of experience. Most of the fathers in my neighborhood growing up were either drunks, abusive, a womanizer or a combination of all of them. Being a father during the seventies was definitely different than being a father today.

After having so much difficulty trying to reach David I decided to take a break and then focus on trying to reach Tracey. Tracey was on my side of the country so I figured maybe I could reach out to him and speak about these new findings. Maybe he would be easier to reach. Besides, I was on a mission to find all my siblings, so it really didn't matter which order I found them in. Darryl told me that he hadn't spoken to Tracey since our father's funeral, but he diwould try and find a way to contact him. What was the worst he could say, I don't want to be bothered?

As I found more of my siblings I learned that rejection was something I was going to have to get used to. Not everyone was going to care or want to get to know their siblings or relatives. I guess for some people it's out of sight, out of mind. Darryl did manage to contact Tracey, but he proved to be just as complicated as our father.

Tracey

Trying to locate Tracey proved to be more difficult at first than trying to reach David, but Darryl eventually managed to find way to. It was almost as if Tracey was deliberately trying not to be found or contacted by anyone. What was this guy trying to hide?

According to Darryl the last time he spoke to Tracey was when he came to California in 1994 for our father's funeral. Darryl said our father had started to get sick around the late eighties and Tracey had come to California once before our father passed away to visit.

After about a week Darryl contacted me and said he had found a phone number and address for Tracey. Apparently he was now living in New Jersey. I was relieved that he found a contact number and information but figured it would be best if he contacted Tracey first because he knew Darryl was his brother. I figured if I were to contact Tracey I would just be some random stranger claiming to be his brother. Darryl understood my point and agreed to contact Tracey. I patiently waited to see what the outcome of that call would be.

The next day Darryl contacted me and told me about his conversation with Tracey. I must admit it wasn't what I had expected. Darryl said that when Tracey answered his phone he identified himself to him. The next words out of Tracey's mouth were, "how did you get this number?" A weird response from a guy to his brother that he hasn't spoken to in years. Darryl stated that after he told Tracey why he contacted him Tracey's attitude didn't improve. Darryl did say that before they hung up Tracey told him to have me call him the next day at 4 p.m. After their conversation Darryl said he didn't want to have anything else to do with Tracey. From what I knew of Darryl he is an easy-going guy so for him to say that must of took a lot.

Now that I had Tracey's contact number I was a little apprehensive about calling him. If he treated a brother that he knew like that how would he treat me? I had already come to far down this path to stop now so I was going to make that call regardless of the outcome. I said to myself maybe there were some issues between Darryl and Tracey that I didn't know.

The next day I called Tracey at the time he had specified and waited for him to pick up his phone. My guards were already up and on defense just in case the call went sideways. When Tracey answered the phone I identified myself to him. When he spoke the tone in his voice said it all. I could tell that this was going to be a short call, and I really had no hopes of gaining anything useful from it. I knew I probably had one shot at connecting with him, so I went for it.

I explained to Tracey that my mother had concealed the identity of my biological father from me my entire life and I just became aware of it a few months ago. I said to him I know this is as much of a shock to everyone as it is to me, but I'm just trying to get some answers so that I can get to the truth. I explained to him that I was not trying to intrude or upend anyone's life, I was just looking for some answers. I don't know what it was but for some reason that seemed to connect with him. His voice became less defensive as he started to speak about how he could relate to my mother being dishonest with me because his mother was also dishonest with him. I didn't know what that meant at the time, but I eventually found out and it wasn't pretty.

After what seemed like a brief moment of bonding Tracey said, "Are you sitting down? I have some news that is going to knock you off your feet." I said to him, I just found out about seven siblings I never knew existed, what else could be more shocking than that? That's when he told me that we have another sister.

Another sister? I was like what? This now makes eight siblings. My first thought was, when is this going to end?. How many kids did William have? The more siblings I found out about the more this was beginning to sound like an episode of Jerry Springer. Things got even weirder when he told me her name, Diane Burton. I said to him, Diane Burton? I know who that is. I didn't know her personally, but she lived in the neighborhood that I grew up in and I would see her from time to time. She was familiar with a lot of kids in the neighborhood because her adopted mother was a popular lunch lady at a local school.

Now images of seeing her when I was younger started to run through my mind. I would see her outside in passing but that was about the extent of it. I was like this is unreal. I had been seeing my sister in passing for years and never knew she was my sister. What came out of Tracey's mouth after that was even stranger. He told me that her married name is Pierce and that her husband was Terrence. That was a name that I knew also. I didn't know Terrence personally, but I knew of his brother who was a fireman in the same town as me. As a police officer we routinely collaborate with the firemen on calls. What a small world I thought.

Tracey then said that I could find her on Facebook, but I was on my own from there. That didn't make any sense that he wasn't going to get involved with introducing me to our sister. I was like, "why wouldn't my brother want to introduce me to our sister?" I sensed there was more to this, but I was probably going to have to speak to Diane in order to find out. His strange behavior about Diane had me wondering if I even wanted to know her.

I didn't want to push the conversation any further, so I just ended it there. I said to myself that maybe he would warm up later on and talk to me some more about our family. Before we ended the call I thanked Tracey for taking the time to talk to me and providing me with the information. I told him that I would definitely reach out to Diane. Two days later I texted Tracey to thank him for the time he took to speak to me the other day, but by now he had turned that phone number off. When I told Darryl what had happened he also tried to reach Tracey, but he got the same message as me that the phone had been turned off. I don't know about anybody else, but I can take a hint.

Contacting a woman as a complete stranger seemed creepy and weird to me, but I had to do it. I sat back and took some time to think about which way would be best in approaching this awkward situation. I knew I wasn't going to get any assistance from Tracey, so I had to come up with something good.

When I spoke to Darryl after my phone conversation with Tracey I found out yet another discovery. Tracey had never told Darryl or David about our sister Diane. As far as we know he never told our father about her either. I later found out that our father had thought Diane died at birth because that is what Tracey's mother had told everyone. What would he have thought if he found out that his daughter survived? There was something odd about Tracey that I just couldn't put my finger on.

If I had to guess I would say it was his mother's influence. I learned later from Diane that Tracey was close to his mother, and he would never do anything to alienate her. It was now time to reach out to Diane and get her version of this story.

Diane

I knew contacting Diane was going to be awkward. I knew of her from my younger years, but I didn't know her personally. Most likely she probably wouldn't recognize my name. How do you contact someone out of the blue on social media and tell them that you are their older brother without sounding like some kind of crazy internet creep? I had to carefully think this one out. I probably was only going to get one shot at this, and I had better make it good. It took several days before I got up the courage to message Diane. I was still thinking about the strange way Tracey had told me about her and how he didn't want to have anything to do with helping us connect. I had no idea what to expect. Was she strange, weird or was it something else? Tracey's actions made it hard to tell.

I couldn't stop thinking about the way Tracey had ended our conversation by turning off his phone so I couldn't contact him again. I didn't let it bother me because I came into this with no expectations.

Upon checking Facebook, Diane's profile was on there just like Tracey had said, but it offered little information. After much thought I decided to send her a message. I said to myself that whatever I wrote it would have to be something that peaked her attention and was unique. It had to be something only someone who was really family would know.

I took a deep breath and proceeded to type my message to her. This was going to be do or die. I started out by mentioning Tracey and explaining to her that I had spoken to him recently and that he told me how to reach her. I then asked her if her father was William Lee Felton. Obviously, that was all she needed to hear. Diane responded back with a message asking if I could call her. Before I could say yes, she quickly messaged me her phone number for me to call her. Now I was feeling a little more at ease knowing that she took me seriously and didn't write me off as some crazy person or scammer.

After a brief pause I finally dialed Diane's phone number. Not knowing what to say, I just decided to give it to her straight. By now this speech was starting to sound like some prerecorded line from a desperate telemarketer trying to get a sale.

So far the odds were working in my favor. Three of the four siblings were very warm and welcoming, which made it easier and more comfortable for me to talk about this. I've always been the type of person to keep my business to myself, but with my siblings my business was their business too. Besides, after fifty years of holding in a secret it finally felt good to let it all out.

After running down my story to Diane, I wasn't prepared for the story she was about to tell me of her life. Diane told me she was adopted at birth by an older couple who had lost their biological daughter at twenty-one years old to asthma. Diane said she did not learn of her biological parents until she was twenty-five years old. I thought children get adopted all the time, so this isn't anything strange, but the story of Diane's adoption was. Diane and Tracey had the same biological mother and father. When William and Cheryl separated after the birth of Darryl, Cheryl was already pregnant with Diane. William and Cheryl's divorce was finalized in December of 1965, but Diane wasn't born until February of 1966. Diane was born prematurely with health issues which probably only added to the trauma that Cheryl was going through. All alone, Cheryl quietly gave birth to Diane at the hospital, but the story she told everyone afterwards would later prove to be devastating. Cheryl told everyone that Diane had died at birth in the hospital when in reality she didn't. I'm sure Cheryl was not the first nor last woman to tell such a dreadful lie, but those types of lies can one day come back to haunt you.

Diane was born two months prematurely in Waterbury, Connecticut in February of 1966. It was believed that Cheryl may have given birth early due to the anxiety and stress that she was going through due to her recent divorce from William. According to the doctor's notes when Diane was born, Cheryl's outlook on life had become very bleak by this time. A single mother with three children and no husband, Cheryl probably could not bear to take on the responsibility of raising a third child that had potential health issues. Under those circumstances I don't think anyone would have looked down on her if she had just told the truth. Diane not only represented another liability, but she probably reminded Cheryl of the tumultuous relationship she had with William and the circumstances of how she was conceived and how her marriage ended. To add to the issues Cheryl was informed by the doctors that due to the stress and premature birth of Diane there was a possibility that Diane might suffer from some developmental issues. With no husband and three children, Cheryl did the unthinkable, she faked the death of Diane. Upon giving birth Cheryl abandoned Diane at the hospital and told everyone that she had lost the baby at birth, a secret that would come back to haunt Cheryl many years later. It was later discovered that William was never informed that his daughter had survived. William most likely went to his grave not knowing the truth about his daughter and thinking that Diane had died at birth.

It gets even worse. Later, after meeting up with me Diane showed me her adoption papers. I couldn't believe what I was reading. The doctors basically labeled her borderline retarded and said she was good for adoption to a family with minimum expectations. Maybe it was just me, but I think during that time doctors and society just had a low opinion of Black people in general and labeled us as such. I can only imagine how many other children got stereotyped like we did but didn't make it through the system.

As bad as this may sound, this might have been the best thing that could have happened to Diane. One could only imagine the environment Diane may have been raised in if Cheryl had decided to keep her. If the life that Kim and Tracey lived was any indication, Diane too would have been part of a dysfunctional family, and her life could have suffered the same consequences. Although Diane was abandoned and eventually adopted, she was adopted by a loving couple that lived in the same town as her biological mother and siblings. This should have never happened because there were adoption rules that dictated how far away an adopted child had to be in order to get adopted. Maybe this was a mix up in the system or it could have just been pure fate.

Growing up Diane remembered seeing her biological mother over the years because she traveled in some of the same circles as her with her adoptive mother. Through all those years Diane never knew she was in the presence of her biological mother. It wasn't until Diane became an adult and was seeking out her biological parents' information that she realized her biological mother was in front of her the whole time.

Diane often wondered how her biological mother could act like she was a stranger when she saw her knowing that she gave birth to her. Did this woman not have a soul or a conscious?

Diane's discovery of her biological parents only left more questions than answers. When Diane met Tracey for the first time, neither of them knew they were siblings. Diane said they met in a bar one evening where Tracey was a DJ. Diane said they had a short conversation, but something seemed weird about Tracey. Tracey kept telling her that she reminded him of his deceased sister Kim. Diane stated that this seemed awfully strange for him to make this kind of a reference, and she ended their conversation quickly. It wasn't until later after that encounter that they both would find out the truth. Sometimes fate does have a way of stepping in.

Finding out you had an older sister whom you resembled and then finding out she had died before you could meet her can be devastating. A few years after Diane's first encounter with Tracey she finally met him and their mother as a family. Diane thought her biological mother and sibling would be glad to know she was alive and well, but this was far from the case.

Cheryl now had to confront a child who was known by everyone to be dead and a twenty plus year old lie that was about to blow up in her face. Tracey also was forced to deal with the lie his mother had told him his entire life about his younger sister dying at birth. Now what Tracey said to me on our phone conversation about his mother lying to him made sense.

After hearing all of this I wanted to meet the sister whom I never knew existed. We seemed to share a lot in common and we were both seeking answers. From my conversation with Tracey, he did tell me that our deceased sister was buried in Waterbury, CT. When I mentioned this to Diane she confirmed it and told me that she knew where our sister's grave site was. Believe it or not our deceased sister was buried across the street from where I live,

I couldn't believe it. At that time, we made plans to meet up the next day at the gravesite to meet and see our sister's grave site.

When I arrived at the graveyard Diane was already there waiting for me. It was difficult to explain what I felt. After learning about all of these siblings I was finally going to get to meet one face to face. I was thrilled and nervous all at the same time.

When I got out of my vehicle she was standing there with a big smile on her face. It was like we had known each other all of our lives but just never met. She felt like family to me instantly. We hugged and just took in the moment. My whole life flashed before me. The deception and lies my mother had given me. The loss of time not knowing my siblings. The feelings of rejection and abandonment. We both shared these kind of feelings. I was so excited that I had to get a picture of this moment. Luckily for us there was an elderly couple visiting at the graveyard so we asked them if they would not mind taking a picture for us. We told them that we were siblings, and this was the first time we had ever met. The couple congratulated us and was more than happy to take our picture. This was a very special moment for both of us.

After taking the pictures we proceeded to our sister Kim's gravesite. After walking for a while we finally came upon her grave marker which had gotten covered over by grass. Seeing Kim's gravesite and reading the inscription on the marker brought about some feelings I had never experienced before. Why did I all of a sudden become sad over someone I never met? I just felt as though I had a sister that I had never met and would never get the chance to know. It was saddening but yet real. My mind was trying to envision what kind of person she was or would have been, what type of personality did she have, what kind of relationship we would have had? It was a solemn moment and also a moment of closure for me. We stayed for a little while, silently, as this moment sunk in for both of us. Diane had already been to Kim's gravesite several times before this day, so it wasn't as dramatic for her as it was for me. Diane and I talked for a little while before leaving the gravesite. I told her we will definitely talk more later after I have had some time to let this all-sink in. After saying our goodbyes, we both drove off and let this moment sink in.

As Diane and I got to know each other we shared many memories of our childhoods. Diane told me how the Black girls didn't like her in Catholic school, and she was constantly running away from fights with them. Now Diane was no small, frail girl that couldn't have defended herself. She was tall and fit and was an athlete in school who could have easily beaten most of these girls up, but she just wasn't that type of person. A funny story she shared with me was how these mean girls denied her application to join the Afro American Club in school. Now don't quote me but I'm pretty sure the only requirement to join a club like that is to be Black. Good thing we didn't know we were siblings at that time because I would have shown those girls just how Black I was.

Now that I had been bombarded with a ton of new information, I knew there was probably much more to go. As I was learning about all these new siblings I still didn't know much about the man at the center of it all, so I decided it was now time to learn more about the father that I never knew, William Lee Felton.

William Lee Felton?

It's 2024 and this year marks thirty years since his passing. William Lee Felton, aka Bubbles, was a complicated man with a penchant for women. I'm not insinuating that he was a player, but he did have his fair share of women. Usually when William's relationship with a woman soured, so did his relationship with their children. However, there was something different about William. Normally when men have a lot of children by different women they usually didn't have a serious relationship with the mothers, but William did. All except for my mother as far as I know. It could be that he truly wanted a relationship with these women but was just incapable of sustaining a healthy one. As women call it he was a hopeless romantic.

At this time, I was dealing with limited information, but it was enough to create a partial profile of the father I never knew. As the years went on I learned much more about William and gained a certain respect for him. I learned that he wasn't a perfect man, but he wasn't a bad one either. To get a true sense of who he was I had to look at things from the way they were when he was growing up.

In essence we are all a product of our environment, subject to its influences.

William Lee Felton was born in November of 1942 in Hobbsville, NC. He was the third child of William Roy and Sennia Roberts Felton. William had two sisters, Lillian, and Edith Faye. His older brother, James, died during his first week of birth. James would have been the eldest child. William came from a poor Black farming family in the heart of North Carolina. After World War II there was a period of economic hardship amongst everyone. To better understand the environment of North Carolina at that time you must look deeper into its past.

The reconstruction era, 1865 to 1877, was a period of military occupation. With enfranchisement of formerly enslaved people, who allied with the Republican Party, a biracial legislature was elected. It established public education and welfare institutions for the first time in the state and initiated economic programs. Reconstruction ended in 1877 after white Democrats, known then as Dixiecrats, regained political control of the state through violence and intimidation at elections. They passed new laws and constitutional amendments that disenfranchised Black people and many poor Whites near the turn of the century. In the Jim Crow era, from the late 19th century to 1964, Black people were suppressed as second-class citizens, nearly excluded from all politics. To escape the segregated south thousands of Black people migrated north to escape the harsh conditions which were associated with violence and murder. The state was predominately rural, with an agricultural economy and all residents of the state suffered in the Great Depression of the 1930s.

The many training bases and munitions plants established in World War II stimulated the economy and provided some new opportunities for Black people during this time, but this did nothing to fix the injustices which had already been sewn into the American culture. State integrated public facilities were ushered in by Dr. Martin Luther King Jr. during the broad-based activism of the Civil Rights Movement in the 1950s and 1960s. After 1950, the economy grew and became more diverse, with cotton receding in importance. North Carolina started to see some improvements but hardly enough. This was a time of high migration to the north by Black families seeking better living wages, equal rights, and a better quality of life, but the north wasn't without its problems too. Many northern Whites may not have supported slavery, but a lot didn't believe in integration either. You could look at a map of the sundown towns in the north to figure that out. Maybe that's where the phrase "separate but equal" came from.

By the 1950's William's parents had moved from Hobbsville, North Carolina to Plainfield, New Jersey to seek better opportunities. Not long after their arrival William's parents' relationship started to sour. When William was about ten years old his mother left his father and moved the family to Waterbury, Connecticut where she had family members. William Roy stayed behind and eventually became a truck driver before he moved back to North Carolina where he stayed until his passing. Very little is known of William Roy because he didn't stay in touch with his wife and children. I did find out that William Roy had two daughters born in Plainfield, NJ after the separation. You could say my father followed in his father's footsteps.

William's mother chose Waterbury, Connecticut because she had family members in the area who had also left the south hoping for a better life. William's mother figured the move would give her the closure she needed from her ex-husband and the chance for her children to have a better life, removed from the still segregated south and her ex-husband. There are those who chose to believe differently but events in our lives can have a significant effect on our families for generations to come. Africans were forced to come to this country against their will and then enslaved for hundreds of years, stripped of their identity, forced to work for nothing and suffered from rape, mistreatment, and murder. How could any rational person not believe that this would have a long-lasting effect for many years to come for African American people?

Growing up during the sixties was difficult. Race relations were at an all-time high and African Americans were fighting two wars. One against society and the other against their own race. While growing up, William's parents had always told him and his siblings that they could be anything they wanted to be. I suppose this was his parents' way of challenging him and his siblings to be better and do better than they had done. Now it was their responsibility to meet the challenge. Unfortunately, society had a different view on this challenge. Society's take on it was you could be anything you wanted to be as long as you knew where your place was.

In 1960 William graduated from Croft High School in Waterbury, Connecticut. A star football player, he was also very popular amongst the ladies. My mother migrated to Waterbury, Connecticut from Saluda, South Carolina with her family after her high school graduation in 1958. As I later found out, William also played football and graduated with two of my mother's close cousins. I tried to talk to one of the cousins about my father, but that conversation went nowhere. He is very loyal to my mother, and it was clear that he didn't want to overstep his boundaries by saying anything. The more I think about it the more I don't believe my mother meeting William was random. I believe she knew him before he was married.

In March of 1963 William married Cheryl and their first child was born in April of 1963, Kim. Kim was the first of many children for William. As with most marriages I'm sure it started out fine at first but quickly started to deteriorate. It didn't take long however for William to start wandering because I was conceived in May of 1963. I don't know if my mother knew he was married or just didn't care, but she was determined to hide his identity from me and everyone else. I can't say for certain, but I don't think my mother ever told William that she was pregnant with his child. This was a revelation that totally changed my whole mindset about him. How could I be angry with my biological father if he never knew I even existed? William moved to California with Dixie and their son Darryl in 1966, but by 1967 William had a total of six children in Connecticut and California.

In August of 1967, my brother David was born in Anaheim, California. A year later in 1968 William enlisted in the US Army at age twenty-six and was deployed overseas during the Vietnam War. This seemed a little strange to me that the military would take a mother's only son, who also had a newborn child, and enlist him and ship him out on active duty overseas. This meant he left his live-in girlfriend with two small children to raise while he was gone. Maybe he did it for financial reasons, who knows. William served eleven months and eighteen days in the Army. He was overseas in Vietnam for six months and three days. He served as a private first class E1 before he was honorably discharged for personal hardship.

During his service William worked with missiles and rocket launchers while enlisted in the Army.

Trying to figure things out after the fact is always challenging. Most of the people who would have had the answers that I was seeking are either deceased, wouldn't talk or are suffering from Dementia or Alzheimer's disease. If I had just been aware of who my biological father was twenty years sooner I could have gotten many more answers to my questions.

My mother must have kept her relationship with William secret because no one I talked to even knew they had one. Getting low on resources I started looking to other avenues for information. After a long illness William passed away in November of 1994. I heard he had Lupus and COPD, but it could have been something related to his service in Vietnam, possibly agent orange. William's sister, Edith Faye, had passed away also in January of 1994 in a house fire. Her only child, Chad, also perished in the fire with her. The thing about Edith is that we knew each other. As a child my mother's brother use to date her. She would come by my house with my uncle and even spoke to me on several occasions. Neither of us knew that we were related as my mother just stood by and watched silently.

William's older sister, Lillian, passed away in 2012. She was predeceased by her daughter, Carolyn. Lillian did, however, have a son named Robert aka Breezy. Robert was definitely someone I wanted to talk to because he was close in age to my father, and he could give me some good insight into his life seeing that he use to hang out with him. My cousin Bobby was also a military veteran.

Several years after moving to California William and Dixie split up. After the split William went on to have three more daughters by three different women during the mid-seventies, early eighties. Other than an infidelity problem and possibly anger issues fueled by a drinking problem, William seemed very much like an ordinary man with flaws.

One thing was very obvious though. Although he had many children, all except me were from relationships that he was in. He wasn't just having a bunch of kids from one-night flings. It doesn't excuse his infidelities, but it does make him look a lot more human. I'm hoping I'm not speaking too soon and find out there is another batch of William's kids out there.

This information gave me some insight into the early years of William's life. I didn't want to say his name without understanding who he might have been. As time went on I learned many things about my father. He went to college, he belonged to a Motorcycle Club called The Zodiacs, and he was a Mason.

I would come to find out that there were many sides to him. William's nickname in his motorcycle club was Tight Eyes. I'm assuming he got that name from the way he would squint his eyes. Growing up in a motorcycle club I was well aware of the club names that members had and some of the reasons for why they had them..

As I looked through my father's old photo albums I saw many pictures of Bobby and my father together during their younger years. It was obvious that they hung out so my next step would be to locate Bobby and see if he could, or was willing to, offer me any new information on the father I never knew. I realize that we are all family, but we are also complete strangers as well. As I located people I always kept that in mind so that I didn't overstep any boundaries with anyone. For me this is all new, but for others it could be old wounds being reopened.

Cousin Bobby

Again, here I am about to make my sales pitch. Every time I confronted someone with my story I felt more and more like a sleazy door-to-door salesman trying to sell some cheap products. Unfortunately, you have to start somewhere and what better place than from the beginning. After getting Bobby's phone number from Darryl, I proceeded to contact him. Not wanting to be awkward I asked Darryl if he could call him first and give him a heads-up that I would be calling.

I felt comfortable calling Bobby, unlike the cold introduction I had to do with Diane. After dialing his phone number, I patiently waited until he answered the call. When Bobby answered I could already tell that I liked him. He was warm and friendly and had no problem answering questions about my father. Bobby was ten years the junior of my father, but he did hangout with him a lot before my father moved to California. As with everyone I spoke to, I tried not to bombard him with too many questions up front.

It's been a long time since my father passed away and some people need time to recall some of their memories.

Bobby stated that my father never mentioned anything to him about having another son. When I sent Bobby a picture of my mother he didn't remember her either. I was beginning to believe that whatever type of relationship my mother had with William wasn't out in the open. When I told Bobby about my mother saying William's nickname was Bubba that's when he corrected me. He said my father's nickname was Bubbles. I was like Bubbles. Do you mean like Michael Jackson's monkey? He said yes, but he didn't know why or where the name came from. My mother is notorious for mispronouncing names so this seemed about right for her to call him Bubba. Later I would see in my father's yearbook that he listed Bubbles as his nickname so this must have been a name that he had since he was a little boy.

As our conversation continued I found out that Bobby actually lives in my neighborhood just like Diane. Bobby also told me about his sister, Carolyn, who had died at an early age. I had close family members living right around the corner from me all these years and I never knew it. At this point I decided to keep our conversation short but asked if it would be alright for me to call another time and talk more. Bobby said he would like that very much. When we hung up I smiled and was glad to have such compassionate and understanding family members.

With six siblings down there were only two more left to find. Finding Ave and Keisha would prove to be the most difficult because there was very little known about either of them. Even if I did find them, who knows how much they would even know about our father. Besides, William did have a track record of having children and burning down relationships.

The Lost Sisters

Finding the last two sisters was going to prove to be the most challenging. After much research and fact finding, it became clear that finding Ave and Keisha was not going to be that easy. Darryl stated that he had not seen Ave since our father's funeral, and he has no idea where Keisha could be. Diane agreed to help out as she searched the internet and social media for any signs of our lost sisters.

By this time Darryl had sent me more information and pictures of our father for me to analyze. One of those items was our father's funeral program. Upon reading it there was a beautiful tribute written about our father in it and the writer was Ave. It appeared that she had great memories of our father, and she loved him very much. This even further helped me to understand who William Lee Felton might have been. He may have had some bad traits, but he also had some good ones. I remember an old saying that said, "No one is actually dead until the ripples they cause in the world die away." Sir Terry Prachett.

Through my research I found out that both sisters were born in the Los Angeles area. I could find signs of their existence but no solid leads. Keisha would have been the oldest of the two being six years older than Ave.

It was imperative for me at this point to find these last two siblings. I didn't come this far to leave the story open. I had already come this far so there was no turning back. I must admit I did get discouraged a few times, but I continued my search. It was apparent that when William's relationship ended with the women so did his relationship with their child making it that much more harder to locate them. This seemed to be the case for all except Dixie. For whatever reason he always seem to have some sort of a relationship with her even after they had broken up.

Finding these two sisters was crucial for me. I knew that my story would not be complete without them. If either of them knew anything about my father it would give me a closer view of what kind of person he was later in life. After months of trying to locate these two sisters with no success I decided to take a step back to rethink my efforts. I said to myself, if it is meant to be they will eventually appear, you just have to have faith.

After months of searching, I got a phone call at work one night from Diane. Diane was excited as she told me that she had Ave on the other line on the phone. Ave called Diane because Diane had sent out a postal letter to the last address she had for Ave, and it eventually made its way to her. I was eager to speak to Ave because I almost didn't believe we were going to find her.

When Diane clicked over I introduced myself to Ave. When Ave spoke, I told her that she was a hard person to find. Upon speaking to Ave, I proceeded again with my sleazy door to door salesman line of how all of this came about. I told Ave that she was the baby of us all and there was only one more sister to find. Like the rest of us Ave too had siblings on her mother's side that she grew up with but did not know all of her siblings on her father's side. We talked for about a half hour or so before exchanging pictures and hanging up. Ave seemed thrilled to find out that she was the baby of us and that she had other siblings. She knew about Darryl, David Tracey, and Tiffany but not the rest of the siblings. It's strange how Tracey knew about most of the siblings but never shared that information with any of them. Before hanging up I told Ave I would call back another time when it was more convenient for us and then we could talk more about our family. I told her it is easier for me to answer questions when I am at home because I have all of my research work there.

After talking to Ave, I felt more optimistic that we would eventually find Keisha. A few days had passed before I tried to call Ave back but when I did I was shocked to find out that she too had blocked her number. I couldn't believe it. Was it done by accident I thought? If it wasn't then what did I do? This had happened to me before with Tracey, but it still didn't make it feel any better. When I contacted Diane I told her what had happened to me when I tried calling Ave. Diane couldn't believe it either. Diane then said let me try calling her to see if she had been blocked also. After a few minutes Diane called me back and said that she too was also blocked on Ave's phone. Neither of us could understand it. If she didn't want to have a relationship with us all she had to do was say so. Diane did say that when she was trying to find Ave she did see a lot of aliases and different addresses for her. Maybe she's running from something. I'm not going to try and pretend that I can understand everything that is going on in people's lives, but at least she knows where to find us if she ever does change her mind and wants to have a relationship with her siblings. Now we just need to reach Keisha. One down, one more to go.

July 2022

After two years of research, tracking down leads, speaking to family members and friends and many hours of soul searching, I decided to author this book. I created the outline in nine days with all the information I had available to me at the time. I choose to do this in nine days because it reflected one day for each sibling although I knew it would take much more than nine days to complete the story. I couldn't help but to wonder if we had known about each other earlier in life would things have been different and how?

We can't change the past, but we can reflect on it and learn from it to make a better future. As with most stories this one is far from over. Not only did the discovery of my biological father uncover some very old hidden secrets, but it also unveiled other family secrets that my mother had kept from me. As the saying goes, that which was once in the dark will soon come to the light.

To this day the women who participated in my father's life are still carrying the emotional scars from their relationship with him. Most refuse to address it or let it go.

Sometimes letting go of the past is not so simple for some. This may have closed the chapter about identifying my siblings, but for me there was much more to find out. Not only did my mother withhold the true identity of my biological father, but she also hid the identity of her father, my grandfather, from me. Why would someone work so hard to bury secrets? Is there something that I'm missing, or did she just feel that it wasn't important? These are questions that only my mother can answer, but probably never will.

I saved my story for the end because I wanted to recap on the things that lead me up to this point. If you had said forty years I would be authoring this story I would have thought you were crazy, but it was my life and there is nothing that I can do to change the past, but I can change the future. There is still much more to learn and hopefully by the time I'm ready to print this book I will have more answers and will be able to include them in this edition.

Talking about this has brought a sense of peace upon me that I never thought I would have had. With solitude comes peace, with peace comes joy and with joy comes possibilities.

I still wonder how many other people have or are going through situations like this? Looking for that peace of mind that always seem to be eluding them but remaining strong and keeping up a good front to the rest of the world.

My Story

It was once said that every man is either trying to live up to his father's expectation or trying to make up for his father's mistakes. I believe there is some truth to that. Growing up I always told myself that I would not be the man that I thought my father was. The only problem is my father was not the man whom I thought. It worked out though because it just made me be a better all-around person.

In February of 1964 I was born in Waterbury, Connecticut to a single mother living with her grandmother. It took many decades before I found out the true identity of my biological father, William Lee Felton. For decades, my mother had people under the impression that my father was a man named David Riddick.

I don't know if William had any real feelings for my mother. I don't know if their interaction was an opportunity for William to be with another woman. I don't know what my mother's motivations were. Did she know he was married and didn't care? Did she think he would leave his wife to be with her? Was it just an opportunity for her as much as it was for him?

Whatever the reasons were my mother felt it was worth burning down her relationship with her oldest child to keep it buried. As I found out more and more about my father and his life, it was starting to become clear that he never knew my mother was pregnant with his child or even that he had another child. I could think of a few reasons why my mother may not have wanted anyone to know about her affair with William, but that was no excuse for her not telling him that she was pregnant with his child. From all of my research William may have had a lot of children, but he never denied that any weren't his.

As I uncovered more information I found out that not telling the baby's father that she was pregnant was something that was common for my mother. My stepfather revealed to me that after they were married, and my mother got pregnant with my siblings she never told him that she was pregnant. He said he would notice some signs of pregnancy about her, but every time he asked her if she were pregnant she would say no. She continued these lies until she couldn't hide them anymore. Why would a woman conceal her pregnancy, not once but twice, from her husband? I know my mother so well that she can't hide a lie from me, but when it came to her rationale at times I just couldn't figure her out. Many times, I don't even think she knows why she does some of the things she does. As more information became available, I started to form a story line in my head to explain my mother's actions.

To cover up the embarrassment and humiliation of getting pregnant by a married man, I believe my mother led everyone to believe that she was pregnant by a man named David Riddick.

In order to try and understand any of this I had to go back to the time when this all took place to understand the climate and how things were perceived at that time. My mother, just like Cheryl, would have been judged much differently then as they would have been today.

The sixties were a much different time from today. Today two women being pregnant by the same man at the same time is so common that people don't even blink. It doesn't even draw attention, but in the sixties you would have been labeled a jezebel. You might as well stamp a giant red J on your forehead because you were now considered to be an outcast, a woman unworthy of honor.

My mother would have known this all too well because her mother also was not married when she and her brother were born.

The following is a mixture of facts and speculation, but it isn't hard to believe that this is probably what took place back then. Most of the players are either deceased, incoherent or just refuse to talk, but there's a lot to go by to back this up.

When I was born in February of 1964 my father was still in Connecticut. Apparently he wasn't in a relationship with my mother because he was married to a woman named Cheryl at the time. My mother may not have had anything to do with my father after becoming pregnant by him, but she was keeping tabs on him. My mother was friends with both of his sisters. She even worked with William's oldest sister making it easy for her to know his comings and goings. Secretly my mother may have been in love with William but knew she could only love him from a distance. You could say she probably had a love/hate obsession with him.

Still living at home with her grandmother, my mother named me after her grandfather that helped raise her. However, after I was born speculations started to swirl. Being an unmarried woman raised questions as to the identity of my biological father, questions my mother did not want to answer. By now most people had speculated that David was my biological father. Why, I don't know. For my mother this was fine because it drew attention away from the real father, William. Maybe my mother had another reason for this deception. David was known for being an easy-going guy. He never had any problem shelling out money for his children even if he wasn't involved in their lives. Maybe my mother grifted him by letting him think he was the father when he wasn't in order to get money from him. If that were the case then she couldn't tell William that he was the father of her child. This is a horrible assumption but with my mother anything is possible. Sometimes there are no boundaries that she won't cross to get what she wants.

During this period, a new woman had entered into William's life, Dixie, and things were about to become even more complicated. Cheryl, Francis, Dixie, and my mother all attended the same congregation where everyone knows everybody. In the Black community you couldn't go anywhere without someone asking you, "Who are your people?"

This was common amongst Black people because so many of them had migrated to the north from the south. Having ties to so many women in the same circle was not a good move for William.

William was playing it very close to the chest and he would soon be feeling the heat. Gossip travels fast, especially in a close circle like Waterbury and William's circle was closing in fast and starting to become a ring of fire. Although a member of the same congregation as my mother, William had stopped regularly attending church after he and Cheryl were married. By this time Cheryl was starting to have suspicions about her husband cheating while at the same time Darlene's mother had her own suspicions that David was my father. I don't know if David ever denied these allegations but once a rumor is started it spreads like wildfire, especially in a small congregation.

No one dared confront my mother about my father's identity because she was known for having an explosive temper. One question about my father would draw an angry response from her. My mother used her temper and anger to protect her from the hurt that she was feeling inside. Getting mad was her way of pushing people back from the subject, a response most likely attributed to the rejection she may have received from William. My mother was also a recent transplant from the south and naïve to the ways of the big city, so she had a lot to learn herself. My mother was tall, dark, and beautiful and could have had her choice of many men, but she was the type that didn't like to take no for an answer and was determined to have things her way.

When I came into this world it was under less-than-ideal circumstances, but I had a good upbringing. The secret my great-grandmother had told me when I was a little boy about the identity of my biological father continued to plague me throughout my life. I wish I could say my mother's deception was a onetime thing, but it wasn't. Concealing things just seemed to be something my mother was good at. I was approximately five years old when my mother got married to Leroy, my stepfather. Out of the blue one-day Leroy came to our home and never left. No explanation, no forewarning, no nothing. You would think telling your child that you were married would be important, but obviously my mother didn't think so. But what else could one expect from someone who was as secretive as my mother? Again, the marriage was something my great-grandmother informed me of. If not for my great-grandmother I may have never known anything.

After the marriage, my mother and Leroy moved out of my great grandmother's home, but I remained with my great-grandmother. My reason for wanting to stay was not because I didn't like Leroy or was trying to avoid my mother, but because of my schooling. If I'm going to be totally honest part of it was because of my mother. I never felt the warmth and love from her as I did with my great grandmother and grandparents. Because I was enrolled in a special program for school moving would have meant I wouldn't have transportation to school, plus I would be leaving the neighborhood where all my friends were. Leroy was a great stepfather and still is to this day. Not knowing who my biological father was didn't really affect me because Leroy was more of a father to me than William probably could have ever been. Through this journey to find the truth about my biological father, Leroy has always been there to support me. He encouraged me to find the truth and locate my siblings. After all those years Leroy found out who my biological father was the day I told him. He deserved to know the truth that my mother had denied him.

In the years to follow my mother and Leroy had two children, a girl named Stacy, and a boy named Leroy. Throughout my entire life they were the only siblings that I knew I had. I thought David had kids, but I didn't really consider them siblings at that time. As we got older my relationship with my siblings from my mother became strained. They started to have behavioral issues, and my mother always used me as a way to alienate them. She would say to them things like, "Why don't you try to be more like your older brother?" I repeatedly told my mother not to say those types of things to them because she was going to make them resent me, but as I said earlier my mother was not the type of person that wanted anyone to tell her what to do. This continuous comparison eventually created a rift between me and my siblings which still carries its effects amongst us to this day.

How could a woman be married for decades, to a man who accepted and raised her child as his own yet refuse to tell him who the child's biological father is?

Obviously, Leroy's love for my mother and me was strong enough for him to accept this. Things happen in mysterious ways for a reason.

In retrospect staying with my great grandmother may have been the best decision me and my great grandmother could have ever made given my mother's personality.

Although my mother never abused me, there always seemed to be a coldness about her. Even through her lies, deceit, and misdirection, I would go on to have a good life. I would often avoid the subject of my biological father to others out of shame. This was especially embarrassing for me in school because I went to a school in a rural setting where just about every child came from a home with a mother and father.

This made me feel like the odd child in school and also brought up the feelings of rejection that I had growing up. As a child when others would speak of their father I would wonder, how could someone not want their child? Even through all that negativity, deep down inside I still imagined the day when me and my biological father would eventually meet and talk.

In 1974 when I was ten years old I almost died. A lump had formed on my left arm and was continuing to get bigger and bigger over the months. I was taken to my childhood doctor, Dr. Nunes, and he kept telling my mother that I was fine and that it would eventually go away. As the lump increased in size I became weaker and weaker. Fortunately for me, my family convinced my mother to bring me to another doctor for another opinion. When we arrived at my grandmother's doctor, Dr. Meo, he looked at the lump on my arm, ask them how long it's been like that and then told my family to bring me immediately to the hospital. He said he was calling the hospital right now and they will be expecting me. When we arrived at the hospital they immediately took me in and performed emergency surgery on me. I don't know what the lump was, but I do remember Dr. Meo telling my family that I would have been dead in a few days if they hadn't brought me in. That was my first brush with death but there would be others many years later.

In 1981 I was involved in a motorcycle accident. I remember it like it was yesterday. I got off of school eager to borrow my stepfather's motorcycle to go for a ride. After getting the motorcycle out of the garage at my mother's house, I rode back home to get a jacket before riding to New Haven, Connecticut. As I rode off from the house my neighbor's huge Siberian Husky ran out from in between two cars and struck the front wheel of my motorcycle. The force flipped the motorcycle and sent me sailing in the air. The only thing I remember was laying on the ground and seeing a white Corvette stopped a few feet from my head. That day could have gone really bad for me. Luckily, I sustained only a fractured right hand which required three pins to repair. For some that may have ended their passion for motorcycling but for me it was just the beginning.

In 1985 I was shot in an attempted robbery not far from my home. As I parked my car, me and a friend exited it to go into a local bar. My friend was walking ahead of me, so he didn't see what initially happened. As I was walking I heard a male voice behind me say, "Hey, let me talk to you." I didn't know who he was, so I ignored him and continued walking. Suddenly I felt a hand touch my shoulder. I suspected it was the guy that wanted to talk to me. As I turned around to punch him in the face, that is when he put the gun under my left jawbone. There was nothing I could do. There I was with my fist balled up ready to punch this guy with a gun pressed under my jawbone. This happened so quickly that my friend was unaware of what was going on behind him. As the gunman tried to pull me to the side out of sight from anyone my friend happened to turn around and said, "Hey, what's going on?" That took the gunman's attention away from me for a fraction of a second. That was all I needed to finish the punch that I had already started to the gunman's head.

At that moment I knew I had to go for it. I didn't know if the gun was loaded or not and I wasn't going to take a chance that it wasn't. When the punch landed on the gunman's left cheek he fell back, and I heard the gun go off. Now everyone around knew there was a gun and people started to scatter. When I heard the shot I felt something in my left foot but there was no time to worry about that right now. Everyone was scattering including the gunman. Me and my friend then got into my car and drove off. I'm assuming it was the adrenaline that took my mind off of the pain to my left foot.

Approximately an hour after this incident me and my friend had driven to another bar far from where the shooting had taken place. Luck would have it that the gunman from the earlier incident showed up outside this bar and started firing off some rounds at people outside. Luckily, no one was struck. Within minutes the police showed up and blanketed the area. The police quickly interviewed anyone they could find. When they got to me I told them that the gunman was the guy I had an altercation with earlier that evening. When they asked if I was hurt I said I feel something in my foot but otherwise no, I'm okay.

The officer then asked me to remove my shoe and when I did there was blood inside. I had been shot and didn't even know it. The police then escorted me in my car to the hospital after I refused an ambulance. There they took my clothing as evidence as they continued their investigation. The gunman got away that night but was eventually caught six months later committing another crime. I later found out the gunman was a seventeen-year-old career criminal known for violent crimes. Fate would have it that a few years later I would go on to become a police officer. After that incident I encountered my assailant on a few occasions. He apologized to me for the shooting and asked if we were good. He apparently thought I was holding a grudge and would seek retaliation. A lesser man may have taken justice into their own hands, but I'm not built that way. A few years later he was shot six times in the same neighborhood that he shot me in. Fortunately for him he survived the attack.

As I went through life I had other close incidents with death, but fortunately I lived to tell the tale. I always felt that God looked over me because he had something greater in mind for me. Every day I always looked for what that greater purpose is. Maybe it was to solve this mystery of my biological father, unite my siblings and tell this story. Maybe it's something else that I haven't figured out yet.

In 1989 I became a police officer for the city of Waterbury, Connecticut. For me this was a proud moment. I often wondered that if my biological father were to see me now what would he think? I often picture him saying, "Here is the child that I didn't want to have anything to do with, now look how he turned out." I thought that he would think that despite not caring or being involved in my life I somehow defeated the odds and succeeded in life. At least that's how I pictured it in my head. Once I became a police officer I somehow pushed the thought of that biological father reunion way to the back of my head.

In 1994 I lost several family members and didn't even know it. Not only did I lose my great-grandmother whom I grew up with, but I also lost my biological father, aunt, and cousin. Unfortunately, I didn't know who any of them were at that time because I was still under the impression that David was my biological father.

My great grandmother died at 90 from a heart attack. My biological father's sister Faye and her son Chad had perished in a house fire not far from where I lived, and William passed away after a long illness in California where he resided. William had been ill for a few years before his passing, something I know my mother was fully aware of. Why didn't she tell me when he was sick? I could have at least spoken to him before he passed away. My chance of ever meeting or speaking to my biological father were now gone forever. Three immediate family members gone, and I didn't even know they existed. I still remember how I continued to believe that my biological father was still alive somewhere and that maybe one day he would approach or contact me to talk. The least my mother could have done was tell me the truth so that I could have had some sort of closure, but then again that wouldn't be my mother.

It wasn't until November of 2018 that my mother attempted to give me some type of closure, even if it was only a false sense of closure. David, who was now living in North Carolina and had passed away. I knew nothing of this until I stopped by my mother's home one Sunday in November of 2018.

At that time, my mother told me of David's passing and then pushed his newspaper obituary over to me to read. This was strange because as far as I knew my mother didn't know that I thought David was my biological father. For some reason I'm thinking that my mother planted that false story in my great grandmother's head of David being my biological father because she knew that my great grandmother would eventually tell me.

It wasn't until almost two years after David's death that I would be approached by a woman that changed everything. At this point in time my mother thought she was home free. Most of the people who engaged in this entanglement were now gone and she could carry her secret with her to the grave. How could she had anticipated that after all these years someone would show up and open up this can of worms? My mother was not ready to deal with this.

After learning all of this I knew I had to go to California. That's where my siblings were, it's where my father spent most of his adult life and where he was laid to rest. Everyone knows how I am about flying, but I knew I had to meet my family and visit the grave of the father that I never knew.

Road Trip

In my conversations with Darryl, he had told me about his health conditions and some of the things he has been going through lately. None of us know when it's our time but I was not going to pass up the opportunity to meet the brother who helped me through this journey to find my family. I had already lost too many family members without ever getting to meet them and I wasn't about to pass on this one.

Over the next several months I stayed in contact with Tiffany and Darryl as I planned my trip to California. This was a trip that I never imagined in my wildest dreams I would be taking. I had only been to California once in my life and I had vowed to never go back. It was just something about the environment there that just wasn't appealing to me. I had plenty of invitations to go there from my cousin who is a bodyguard in Hollywood, but I always dreaded the long flight. Maybe now after this trip I will reconnect with my cousin and visit him the next time I go to California.

After arranging the time off from work to make this trip, I told Tiffany and Darryl the date that I would be arriving in California. At this time, I still hadn't heard from David but I figured if he wanted to see me then Darryl would let him know when I was in town. Darryl and Tiffany both seemed just as excited to meet me as much as I was excited to meet them. Now that the reservations had been made I patiently waited until the day that I was to fly out to California.

It was May of 2023 when I flew out to California to meet my siblings. This was a trip I never would have thought that I would be making, yet here I am excited to be doing it. I flew straight through because I am not a big fan of flying with layovers. The seven-hour flight gave me plenty of time to think about what I was going to say when I met them. Normally when I'm on a flight the only thing I am thinking about is when we are going to land, but this time was different.

After the long flight I exited the plane and texted Darryl and Tiffany to let them know that I had arrived. I then proceeded over to the car rental area to pick up the vehicle I had reserved for this trip. I was tired from the flight, and I couldn't wait to get to my room to unwind. My plan was to meet Darryl and his wife the next day after I had rested up and gathered my thoughts. I was about a thirty-minute ride away from Darryl and Tiffany was approximately the same distance. The plan was to visit Darryl and his wife on the first day and Tiffany and her family on the following day.

Just to make sure we were all on the same page I called Darryl and Tiffany to confirm our meet ups. As I laid in my hotel bed my mind kept going back to how this all came about. This whole thing was still very much like a dream to me only it wasn't. One day I had a brother and a sister and in the blink of an eye I added eight more siblings to the mix. I remember one time as a kid when I asked my mother about my biological father she made the remark, "He never did anything for you, I was the one that provided for you." She was wrong. My biological father gave me a family and there is no price tag on that. Knowing that I was only going to be here for a few days I decided to turn in early because I had a busy next couple of days ahead of me.

The next day I woke up around 6 a.m.. I felt refreshed and eager to begin the day. After getting up and getting dressed for the day I went to my rental car and proceeded to a diner I saw on the way in for breakfast. As I sat for breakfast I couldn't help but to keep saying in my head, "This is really happening." After finishing breakfast, I called Darryl just to let him know that I was headed his way. Darryl said that they would be waiting for me.

After the thirty-minute ride I pulled up to Darryl's home. As I parked the car a strange thought entered my mind. I realized there was no turning back now. The day I had waited for so long was now here. As I walked up the stairs to his door I proceeded to ring his doorbell. After a brief moment Darryl appeared at the door. As strange as it may sound he didn't feel like a stranger to me. He immediately felt like the brother that I hadn't seen in a long time. We immediately hugged each other before we proceeded into his apartment. Waiting inside was his wife Michelle. She greeted me and hugged me too just like I was family. There was no way I could imagine a more friendly, cordial meeting than this one.

As I walked into their apartment I couldn't help but to notice the family graduation pictures on the walls. For the next several hours we talked as Darryl caught me up to speed on our father and his childhood with him. The man that Darryl was describing was not the man that I had envisioned. He was very much involved in Darryl's and David's life and even made sure his children knew who their siblings were. This was in total contrast of the man that I envisioned to be a deadbeat who abandoned his children. I had to make the adjustment because the man that I knew as William aka Bubbles was pops to Darryl and our brother David. Darryl was very much involved in our father's life all the way up until he passed away. As we looked through photo albums I visually watched my two brothers as they grew up with our father.

Looking through the photo albums was amazing. I saw photos of my father from childhood up to his last years alive. I saw my brothers grow up as kids to the men they are today. I saw my grandmother and aunts that I never got a chance to know. This was an amazing trip through time, something my mother had stolen from me. My feelings about my father had changed dramatically. The person for whom I once resented I now felt sorry for. Not only did my mother cheat me, but she also cheated my father and all of his family of knowing that I existed. How could I ever forgive her for that? I didn't use my anger to be resentful or to get back at my mother. I used it to motivate me to find the truth, the truth that was hidden from me all these years.

It was now a little after noontime, so we decided to go out and get something to eat. Darryl contacted David and told him to meet us at the restaurant for lunch. I thought, finally I will get to meet David. Initially David was supposed to meet us at the apartment and then follow us to the restaurant but after almost an hour had passed we decided to go to the restaurant without him. After arriving at the restaurant Darryl again called David. According to Darryl, David said he was on his way. After waiting for about twenty minutes for David to show up to the restaurant we decided to order our food without him. During lunch Darryl and I continued to talk about our father and how he was with them growing up.

Michelle met Darryl after our father passed so she never got to meet him. I learned from Darryl that although our father and Dixie broke off their relationship when Darryl and David were young, he still remained active in their lives.

After we finished lunch it became apparent that David was not going to show. Darryl tried one more time to reach David and he said that he would meet us at Darryl's home in a half hour. On the ride back to Darryl's home I felt like pinching myself. I didn't know if this was real or if I was dreaming. Here I am in California with a brother that I never knew existed and my sister in-law. This was feeling more and more like a made for television drama story. It had all the elements. Suspense, drama, twists, you name it.

Upon arriving to Darryl's home, we decided to kick back and watch some television to kill time. Darryl said that when David arrives we will know it. He always has his music blasting in his car for people to hear a block away. After about an hour I heard the music. It was David pulling up. We waited for him to come inside but he never did. Apparently he was outside talking to Michelle's son who was on the porch. David eventually made his way into the apartment and when he walked in the first thing he said was, "Wow, he looks like pops."

As Darryl tried to explain everything to David it was obvious that he was taken back by this moment. David hugged me and asked me questions about my upbringing, which I was happy to share with him. We then went outside to take some pictures to remember this moment. One thing that was obvious however was Darryl's and David's height. So far all of our siblings were tall except Darryl and David. Darryl jokingly said, why did me and David get cheated out of height? It appeared that they got their height from their mom who was also short. Up until this point most of our father's women were on the tall side except for Dixie.

David must have stayed for an hour as we continued to look through more photos. Darryl told David about Diane and even showed him a picture of her and Kim. David was amazed at how close they looked to each other in the pictures. One thing I did notice about David was his ability to remember things wasn't great. Sometimes we had to repeat things several times in order for David to understand. When David left I asked Darryl if maybe David was starting to show signs of Dementia, but Darryl said no. He said it's probably from his other activities, marijuana.

After David had left, me and Darryl went back inside his home and continued to go through the photos that he had from our father's photo albums. As I scanned through the pictures I came upon an interesting discovery. There were several pictures that were taken in Waterbury, Connecticut of people whom I knew. When I asked Darryl if he knew who these people were and where these pictures were taken he said no. I then said to him I didn't think you did because these pictures were taken around my home in Waterbury, Connecticut. Judging by the date in one of the pictures our father traveled in some of the same areas as me during the eighties. Based on the location of some of the pictures it was even possible that me and my father could have crossed paths and never even knew it. This story just got a little stranger. It was obvious that our father was coming back to Waterbury, Connecticut but for how long and why I don't know. His mother and sisters were still there as well as Cheryl and his children with her. Could that have been the reason for his return? It's possible that he was returning because of the lawsuit. Kim had passed away in 1978 and there was a big lawsuit going on over her death that wasn't settled until sometime in the mid to late eighties. This means that my mother probably knew when he was in town. My mother can be a busy body, and she didn't let much pass by her. As I continued looking through the photos I saw pictures of our father and the motorcycle club that he belonged to. Our father was a member of the Zodiac MC out of Los Angeles, California. It was a predominantly Black motorcycle club. Our father's nickname was Tight Eyes, probably because of the way he squinted his eyes at times. I knew about the motorcycle club culture because I grew up in it. My stepfather was the president of his motorcycle club, the Waterbury Chapter of Flaming Knights. It's one of the oldest Black motorcycle clubs in America and I spent a lot of time at the club house. When I became of age I also followed in his footsteps to ride a motorcycle, but I never joined a club. For a man I never knew we did share a few qualities. Even David, the man whom my mother had people believing was my father, also rode a motorcycle. I guess I was destined to ride a motorcycle.

It was starting to get late, so I told Darryl I was going to head back to my hotel room for the evening. Tomorrow I had planned to visit Tiffany and then play the rest of the day by ear. As I was about to leave Darryl gave me some photo albums and told me I could keep them. I tried not to take them because I considered them to be special, but he wasn't going to take no for an answer. Darryl also gave me our father's military duffel bag from when he was in the military.

Words could not express how appreciative I was of this. I told Darryl if he ever wanted to see the pictures again he knows where to find them. I was starting to feel more and more like a part of the family. On the drive to the hotel, I went over my agenda for the next day. My father wasn't buried far from where I was staying so I planned to visit his gravesite first thing in the morning. After that I would head over to Tiffany's house to meet her.

My father was buried in a military graveyard in Riverside, California. It was a beautiful graveyard fully decorated with flags and military ornaments. When I arrived there I went into the office to get the location of my father's grave. The lady behind the desk was very helpful and quickly got me the information that I was looking for including a map to direct me there. After getting the directions to his gravesite I left the office and proceeded to my father's gravesite. When I arrived at my father's gravesite and looked at his marker it was like a big sigh of relief had come over me. This was the closure I was always looking for. Now I knew it was final. My father is dead, and I now know that I will never get to meet or speak to him.

This was weird because this was the second time I had gotten closure from my father's death, but this time it was for real. Standing there looking over his grave I couldn't help but have flashbacks of all the photos and stories that Darryl had shared with me and told me about. Darryl told me that our father said to him, "Don't come to my grave to visit because I'm not there." Hearing that made me realize how important it is to stay in touch with those you care about when they are alive. I guess that's why I was never a fan of going to funerals because I didn't want to remember people like that. I wanted to keep and cherish the moments I had when they were alive.

Before leaving the graveyard I texted Tiffany to let her know I was on my way to see her. I told her that when I was in her area I would contact her first. She responded back saying that she would be waiting. Upon arrival to her neighborhood, I stopped in a nearby plaza and texted her to let her know I was here, but I got no response. I had Tiffany's address, but I don't go to anyone's home without them knowing I was coming first. For the next two hours I tried to reach Tiffany by phone, but she never responded. My first response was worry because I had hoped nothing had happened to her. Unfortunately, that wasn't the case. Tiffany had stood me up. How could someone stand up their brother who had traveled thousands of miles to see them? Me and Tiffany had spoken many times over the years, so I was no stranger to her. I could understand getting cold feet but at least be honest with me and tell me.

When it became apparent that Tiffany wasn't going to contact me I then contacted Darryl and told him I would be heading his way to spend more time with him and his wife. Good thing Tiffany didn't live far from Darryl.

Upon arriving to Darryl's home, he asked me how my visit with Tiffany was. That's when I told him there wasn't one. I told him how I waited around for two hours, and she never contacted me. Darryl was pissed. He couldn't believe she would do something like that considering I had flown all the way her to meet them. Darryl said he was going to call her, but I stopped him. I said let's wait until tomorrow just in case an emergency did come up. I didn't want to jump the gun and assume she ghosted me like that. A lot of people would have been furious about this, but I wasn't because I enjoyed Darryl and his wife's company.

For the next few hours Darryl found more information for me to look at. Darryl found our father's high school yearbook and more pictures for me to look at. Our father graduated from Croft High School, also known as Echo, in Waterbury, Connecticut in 1960. He was a star football player and was part of a football team that had lost no games that season. As I scoured the yearbook I came across some very interesting finds. Two of my mother's close cousins not only graduated with my father but were also on the same football team as him. My mother is close to these cousins making it that much more likely that she knew my father before he was ever married. Unfortunately, the only person alive who can answer that question is my mother. The more I found out the more ties it seemed my mother had with William.

After another great visit with Darryl and his wife I proceeded back to my hotel room to get some rest. I was going to be flying out on a late flight the next day, so I had some time to burn during the day. I always wanted to see the Hollywood sign and the walk of fame, so my plan was to do just that tomorrow.

Hollywood

After getting a good night's rest I woke up and got ready to see Hollywood. This trip was starting to turn out to be more than I had planned. Hollywood had always been on my bucket list of places to go and things to see and now it was going to happen. As I drove down the highway to my destination I took in the scenery like a tourist from out of the country. I couldn't have a picked a nicer day to go to Hollywood.

As I exited the highway ramp I proceeded to drive into town. I had already been forewarned about what to expect so I kept my expectations to a minimum. As I drove through town I couldn't help but feel like I had already been here before. Over the years I had seen so many movies set in Hollywood until now it just felt like I was driving through a huge movie set. I eventually found a place to park and continued my tour on foot.

When people think of Hollywood they think of this fabulous place filled with movie stars, flashy cars, and beautiful scenery when in reality it is a cheap looking trashy dive. As I walked through the streets I couldn't help noticing how trashy the side streets looked and the amount of homelessness there was. It was amazing. Look one way and you see someone drive by in a $500,000 car, look the other way and you see someone living in a beat-up Honda Civic parked on the street. The disparity in wealth was on full display in this town. Like many people, this is a part of society that is so hard to understand. Poor has no limits. It doesn't care about your ethnicity, gender, social status, or anything else. Poor is just poor in its eyes. Unfortunately, some people think poor is different when it affects them. That's when they start looking for others that don't look like them to blame for them being poor. If they ever woke up they would realize just how much we could all gain by working together.

I marveled at the Hollywood sign on the hill. I finally got to see it in person. I walked past Capital Records and strolled on several streets to observe the stars on the sidewalk. I stumbled upon a car show on a side street with some really nice cars. I enjoyed seeing the sights but as far as I was concerned once was enough.

After several hours of taking in the sights it was now time for me to start heading towards the airport to catch my flight back home. As I was walking back to my rental car my phone rang, it was Darryl. When I answered he asked how my sightseeing was going. I told him great. He then went on to tell me that he had called Tiffany, and she answered. He said when he questioned her about not being there yesterday when I went to see her she just said she got tied up.

Darryl said he wasn't buying it. He said she could have at least told you rather than leaving you hanging. I told Darryl it's okay. Seeing him, his wife and David made up for everything. Before leaving Darryl gave me some more pictures and other mementos from our father to take back home with me. This meant the world to me. I knew when I returned home I would have my work cut out for me. I'm sure there is a lot in those pictures that I haven't figured out yet, but I will over time.

As I drove to the airport it was strange, but it felt like I had gone on a pilgrimage to find my past. I now had answers to a lot of questions I had but there were still many more questions to go. I returned my rental car and headed to the terminal to prepare to board my flight. I couldn't wait to get home to talk to Diane and Bobby about what I had learned in California. As I said before my mother is a busy body so I knew it wouldn't be long before she found out about my trip to California. I didn't care. I gave her the opportunity to come clean with me and she didn't. Her reluctance to tell me the truth would only lead me to uncovering even more of her secrets and lies.

The Return Home

Now that I had seen and learned what I went to California for, it was now time to head back home. I must have slept the entire flight back. I guess all that walking and excitement in California had finally caught up to me. After getting off of the plane I made sure to text Diane and Darryl to let them know I had arrived safely. The bond that I now had with Darryl and Diane was amazing. I could feel that we legitimately cared for each other, something I was not accustomed to with my other siblings on my mother's side. From the time that I returned back from California not a day goes by when me and my newfound siblings don't have contact with each other. It's like clockwork. Something will go off and say, "You haven't heard from or contacted your siblings."

When I got home I took a day to unwind before I got back into researching my family history. There was still the question of whatever happened to our grandfather, and did he have any other children after separating from our grandmother? My father's family originated from Gates County, North Carolina. Maybe a trip there could answer more questions.

As an African American your family searches can only go but so far. Prior to the Civil War African Americans were only referred to by numbers and descriptions. African Americans during that time were considered to be property, not human. Our lives were no better than common livestock, use them for what you can get out of them and when they prove to be worthless you get rid of them. This part of my history was not something that I enjoyed learning about, but you can't understand what's going on now if you don't know how it started. This forced me to confront some of the worst atrocities some people inflicted African Americans. There were some records of people who were born prior to 1865, that is if they died after 1865, but any African American who died prior to 1865 were forgotten.

On my second day back, I couldn't wait to tell Diane and Bobby about my trip. I joked with Bobby about pictures I saw of him and my father in California. Back then Bobby was called Breezy. I could tell that he and my father were some suave guys back in those days.

I told Diane how our brothers were amazed at how much she resembled our sister Kim.

Sometimes talking to someone that has gone through something similar eases you and makes you more comfortable to talk about it.

So far it seemed like Tiffany and Tracey were going to be a wash. They didn't seem to want to have anything to do with us and I was not going to force myself upon them. Whatever their reasons are for shunning their siblings I'm sure it makes sense to them. As far as I was concerned it was their loss. They had some great family members and chose not to acknowledge them. I was thankful however for the information that they did provide to me.

By now I had several manilla envelopes full of family info along with information and pictures that were saved on my computer. Sorting through everything was going to take a lot more time but I was ready for it. It seemed as though every time I looked through the information something else would stand out. It has now been four years since Darlene appeared in my life and broke this decades-old family secret.

I would still periodically speak to Darlene by phone, but by now her health was deteriorating rapidly. I could tell in her voice that she was tired and ready to give up. I don't know what it was but even I felt as though Darlene's time was limited.

During this time, I was also getting DNA hits, not just from my father's side of the family, but also from my mother's father's side of the family. This only made matters more complicated because I hadn't fully finished working on my father's side of the family. I decided to look into the DNA hits on my grandfather's side to give my mind a little bit of a break. Besides, Diane and Darryl were also helping to locate our last sister.

As I looked into my mother's father's history, I made an amazing discovery. For all these years I thought my mother's maiden name was Abney, but I found out this was not true. My mother's maiden name was actually Green, not Abney. How could I not even know my mother's real name? It was becoming more and more obvious that I didn't know my mother as good as I thought I did. It was like that Dr. Seuss book "Are You My Mother?" My mother and her brother were raised by their grandparents whose last name was Abney. My mother just adopted their name I suppose. I actually found this out from my stepdad who told me that he didn't even know her birth surname until he saw their marriage certificate. I now had even more questions for my mother which I know she will never answer.

Upon contacting some of the matches on my grandfather's side I was hoping that someone might have a picture of him. I grew up my entire life having a grandfather that I knew nothing about. I spoke to a few older relatives in my family, and they were able to describe him, but no one had a picture. Again, I just couldn't understand why my mother never told me about her father. From what I had gathered my mother was his only child. At first I thought maybe something bad had happened between them and see didn't want to have anything to do with him. I was surprised when I found out that my mother did have contact with him and his family but for some reason excluded me from the mix.

As I further dug into my grandfather's history I found two of his nieces whom I was able to speak to. Upon speaking to his nieces, I was shocked to learn that they knew who I was.

Apparently my mother told them about me but never told me about them. One of the nieces told me that she met me at my cousin's house years ago. As she explained, I remember meeting her but I had no idea she was my relative, let alone my grandfather's niece. She told me that she assumed that I knew who she was through my mother. It seemed like the more I dug the deeper the hole got. None of this was making any sense to me so I knew it wouldn't make any sense to someone hearing this story, but it is what it is. You can pick your friends, but you can't pick your family.

My grandfather lived in Pennsylvania as well as most of his side of the family. I was very familiar with Pennsylvania because I took many trips there with my family as a child. Although my grandfather's family lived close by we would always go to Pennsylvania to visit my mother's side of the family. If my mother wanted to she could have easily brought me to meet my grandfather, but I guess to my mother that wasn't important. I often wonder if it even dawns on my mother about what she did and the effect it had on me.

I now had a father, two grandfathers, a grandmother and eight siblings that I never knew anything about. I'm not suggesting that my life would have been better if I had known them, I'm just saying that I had a right to know them. At this point I was starting to question myself. Why didn't I push harder to find out this information sooner? I guess I just needed someone to push me.

For the next several months I searched to find pictures of my grandfathers and their burial sites but came up blank. I did, however, have pictures of my father's mother. The prospect of ever meeting them was long gone but a picture could help me place an image to the people I would never get to meet. I heard my mother's father was tall, dark skin and had big eyes. A description that also fit my mother. I heard from family members that they use to call him bug because of his big eyes. Unfortunately, I had no one who could give me a description of my father's father. Fortunately, I did get pictures of my father's mother. She looked like your typical warm loving grandmother from the south. I feel that if I had ever gotten the chance to meet her I would have liked her.

Whenever I came to a temporary dead end I would shift directions to work on another part of this puzzle. Sometimes taking a break can help you see things more clearly when you return to them. I doubt I will ever get all the answers I seek but I will never stop trying.

The Lost Sister: Part 2

By now Diane was fully committed to helping me locate our last sister. She scoured social media sites, did Google searches and in a last-ditch effort was going to resort to what worked for finding Ave, a letter through the mail to her last known address. I couldn't understand why it was so hard to locate Keisha. It was almost like she had fallen off the grid and didn't want to be found. If that were the case I could respect that, but if it weren't then I wanted to find her.

One day after months of getting nowhere I received a phone call when I was at work. It was Diane calling to tell me that she had found Keisha. Of all places Diane said she decided to check Instagram, and she found a profile with the same picture that she had gotten of Keisha from someone that knew her. Diane told me that she sent her a message and she is just waiting for her to respond back. Working together is good because I would have never thought to check Instagram or send a letter through the mail, plus it would seem really weird getting a letter from a complete stranger claiming to be your brother. I felt it was something that was better left for a woman to handle.

A couple of days passed before Diane told me that Keisha had responded back to her. She said Keisha told her she was sorry for the delay, but she just needed time to process everything. Finding out you have a bunch of siblings you never knew existed isn't something you hear every day. Diane said they must have talked for about an hour sharing information and trying to get caught up. Diane said Keisha told her that she was in an eighteen-year relationship with her partner and that she was living in Sacramento, California. Keisha told Diane that she is terrible with social media and doesn't really go on there much.

Diane said she told Keisha that I was the one with all the information because it was me who found them when I was researching into my family history. Keisha told Diane that she knew about Darryl, David and Tiffany but didn't know how to reach any of them. However, Keisha was unaware of the other siblings that she had. Diane said that she told Keisha before they hung up that she was going to give her number to me and that I would be getting in contact with her soon. After their phone call Diane forwarded Keisha's phone number over to me.

Eager to hear her voice I called Keisha right away. When she answered I identified myself to her. The moment was joyous as I told her that she had no clue as to how hard we worked to locate her. Again, with my sleazy door to door salesman approach I had to run down my story so that she could somewhat get an idea of how we reached this point. I told her about Tiffany being the first one to reach out to me on Ancestry and about how I was like the rapper Lil Jon when Tiffany hit me with the information of her being my sister. Every time she responded with something I couldn't believe I was like, WHAT!!!, WHAT!!!. But when she responded with something that I could relate to I was like, OOOH Kayyyy!!!.

As Keisha was soon to find out I could be a clown when I wanted to be. We had a really good conversation, and I must admit Keisha immediately felt like family. I was so glad I didn't give up looking for her. I told Keisha it was my goal to try and unite all of our siblings so that we all know who we are and how to find each other. I told Keisha that I had to go now because I was at work, but I would get back to her when I had more time to talk and answer any questions that she may have. Keisha said that she would like that and then we ended our call. I really looked forward to speaking to Keisha again. Seeing this is an ever-evolving story I did some more research on our grandparents so that hopefully I could answer any gaps in our family history. It seemed that most of my siblings didn't even know anything about our grandparents. This is where my detective skills paid off.

Our Grandparents

Our grandparents were William Roy Felton and Sennia Roberts Felton. Both originated from North Carolina and had three children together, Lillian, Edith Faye, and William Lee. A fourth child, James, died within a week of his birth. Sometime during the late forties Roy and Sennia migrated to Plainfield, NJ with their three children. Little is known of Roy and his travels but shortly after moving to Plainfield Sennia left him and moved to Waterbury, Connecticut with their three children. What happened to Roy after that is unknown, but I did later discover that he had two daughters from another woman in Plainfield, NJ.

It was always a speculation of mine that said Roy probably did have more children, but due to the lack of information on him tracking down his history was going to be tough. One day I happened to come across a profile on Ancestry that had a picture of my father's tombstone on it. When I inquired to the poster how they knew him, that is when I found out about Roy's two daughters, Nadine and Stacey

Felton. Apparently this was someone who was close to the daughters and was doing family history research for them. The poster told me that Roy had two daughters by a woman in Plainfield, New Jersey. When I pressed her for more information she said she would talk to the daughters and get back to me. After several days, the poster contacted me and said the sisters didn't have any pictures or additional info on Roy because he wasn't around much when they were growing up. They did say that Roy was buried in North Carolina, but they didn't know the location. Obviously, these sisters knew about my father, but I don't know if my father or his sisters ever knew about them. Sometimes it seemed like the more I found out the more things got tangled. I offered my phone number to the poster for the sisters to contact me, but they declined to take the offer. Rejection was starting to become second nature to me at this point.

Later I spoke to Darryl, Diane and Bobby and told them about the sisters but none of them knew them either. Something did stand out though. Diane said it's a coincidence that these women where from Plainfield, New Jersey and that Tracey had moved to Sicklerville, New Jersey.

I'm thinking Tracey might be aware of our family in Plainfield, New Jersey but just reluctant to share any of that information with his siblings. For me both of my grandfathers were a mystery. I had no idea what they looked like nor where they were buried. Don't ask me why but I just wanted a face to put with the names. I was long past the point of ever getting to know either one of them, so it was more of a curiosity thing.

Finding information on Sennia proved to be slightly easier. Pictures I saw of our grandmother from when Darryl was seven years old showed a heavyset Black woman with a warm smile. It was just a feeling, but I believe if I had ever gotten a chance to meet her I would have liked her. Sennia's parents were the Rev. Edward Roberts and Sennia Hurdle Roberts. Edward was born into slavery in 1854. As I learned and discovered more about my family's history I shared this information with my siblings and cousin Bobby. I don't know what it is but there is something fascinating and liberating about learning about your past. The truth is always better than the alternative.

As I dove deeper into my family history I realized this was way more than my mother hiding a secret for her personal reasons. She deprived me and all of my relatives on my father's side and her father's side from ever getting to know and meet me. They didn't do anything to her so why should they have had to pay the price for what she did? I convinced myself for so long that I didn't care until I actually believed that lie. Darlene may have given me the excuse to look, but I wish I had explored my history a lot sooner when people were alive and could have given me direct answers to the many questions that I have.

Keisha

Keisha was born in June of 1976 in Sacramento, California. Keisha was the seventh child of our father William. As with the many other relationships that our father had, shortly after his relationship with Keisha's mother ended he was gone. Why William chose to have a relationship with Darryl and David and not the rest of his children is beyond me, but he never denied who his children were.

Keisha said that her mother has apologized to her for cutting William off when she was born but they were staying at her grandmother's house with the same phone number and if he wanted to have a relationship with her or talk to her he could have done so easily. Keisha said that her mother said she did try to call William after she was born but another woman who was pregnant by him answered the phone, and she was not very polite. Judging by the time frame this sounded like it would have been Tiffany's mother. Keisha said she told her mother that she had nothing to apologize for, this was all on William. Keisha described her mother as the sweetest most loving mother you could find. Keisha said her mother has to call her every day to check in on her and see how she's doing. According to Keisha when her mother found out we had contacted her she was ecstatic. Keisha said her mother was so glad that she had found her siblings.

I'm not sure why but every time I reached one of my siblings and they told me they were doing good and had a good upbringing it just made me so happy inside. Maybe because I knew society looked down on children born under our circumstances as destined to fail or maybe it's because I knew we faced greater obstacles growing up and yet here we are, we made it.

I've now completed finding all my siblings, at least I hope, but it wouldn't be complete without talking about the one sibling that passed away before any of us even knew she existed. Actually, the only sibling that knew Kim was Tracey. Her story was tragic, and I only wish she could have been alive today to be a part of this reunion.

Kim

Kim is the sister most of us never got to know. She was born in April of 1963 in Waterbury, Connecticut and would have been the oldest of the nine siblings. Kim died in January of 1978 just shy of her fifteenth birthday. Based off information I got from family members who were close to the family, Kim was placed in a hospital at her mother's request for a psychiatric evaluation and later died from medications which were administered to her there. Apparently the hospital prescribed medications to her that caused a reaction that led to her death. A tragic loss for such a young person. This led to a medical malpractice suit being filed against the doctors and Waterbury Hospital.

As I dug deeper into the cause of the circumstances that led to her death it was unclear why Kim was even in the hospital in the first place. From what I heard Kim, and her mother didn't get along very well. Kim was your typical rebellious teenager that didn't get along with her mother. Family members on our father's side said they offered to let Kim come stay with them, but her mother refused to let her go. Maybe Kim would have been here today if she just had let her go. They liked Kim and she got along well with their children. Instead, Kim's mother committed her to a psychiatric hospital claiming there was something mentally wrong with her. That decision would cost Kim her life. To add some clarification to this, Kim's mother was the one that left Diane in the hospital and told everyone that she had died there. I don't know what kind of woman Kim and Diane's mother is, but it was obvious when it came down to her children she seemed to make some pretty bad decisions. I can't help but wonder what effect if any did this have on Tracey? Did he become fearful of his other after what had happened to Kim? Did he think she would do the same to him if he didn't obey her? I don't know.

Upon seeing photos of Kim and Diane their resemblance was amazing. There was no denying that they were sisters. Unfortunately, one was dead literally while the other was dead figuratively. Again, you have to wonder what this did to Tracey. At the age of twelve he had a sister that died at birth, or so he thought, and a sister that died in the hospital unnecessarily. Maybe this explains why Tracey didn't want to get close to any of the rest of his siblings.

Tracey had a weird connection to his mother where he didn't seem to want to do anything to upset her or to get on her bad side. This is probably something only Tracey can answer.

With the passing of Kim that made me the oldest living of the nine siblings. As strange as it may seem when I look at Diane it's almost as if I'm looking at both of my sisters. From the photos I saw Kim looked like your typical happy girl. It's just hard to comprehend her dying so young. I can't help but to wonder if I had ever crossed Kim's path growing up and just had no idea who she was. I did cross Tracey's path when we were younger, but I had no idea that he was my brother. It's probably amazing how many people come in contact with family members every day and do not even know it.

The first time I met Diane face to face we met at Kim's gravesite. I go by there periodically just to pay my respects to the sister I never knew and will never get the chance to meet. I can only imagine what she would have looked like today and what I would have said to her if I got the chance to meet her. RIP Kim.

Aunt Faye

My aunt Edith Faye Felton was born in January of 1944 in Gates County, North Carolina. She was my father's youngest sister and also the feistiest one. Unlike the other family members that have passed away and I never got to meet, Faye's story is different because I actually did meet her. I was a young boy at the time, maybe eight or nine years old when we met. By this time my biological father, her brother, had already moved to California. During this time Faye was dating my mother's brother, Fred. My uncle Fred lived on the third floor in the same building as me and my grandparents and would from time to time stop in before going to his apartment. I was living on the first floor with my great grandmother when I met Faye. I remember a few times when my uncle came in with Faye and they stopped in to see me and my great grandmother. I remember Faye speaking to me with her big smile. She was a tall, pretty dark skin woman that was always smiling. Little did either of us know that she was my aunt, and I was her nephew. It's funny the things that stick in your mind like they just happened yesterday.

According to everyone that I spoke to who knew Faye, the response was always the same. She was loud and always smiling. They said if Faye had anything on her mind she would let you know. This was the polar opposite of my uncle Fred who was a quiet, calm, laid-back person.

Years later after my uncle stopped seeing Faye, Faye had a son, Chad. Chad was born December of 1979. Unfortunately, Faye and Chad both died in a house fire in the winter of January of 1994, the same year my biological father and great grandmother died. According to reports Faye and Chad were both home when a fire broke out in the middle of a winter night. I was unable to find information on the fire, but I speculate that maybe the fire was caused by a furnace issue.

Fortunately for me I was able to locate Faye and Chad's gravesite. They were both buried with Faye's mother, Sennia, in the same graveyard as my sister Kim and other family members.

Many people from both sides of my family are buried in this graveyard that I frequent from time to pay my respects.

My sister Diane also had memories of Faye. She remembers when her adopted mother called Faye and told her that she was alive and well and that Cheryl had lied about her death. Diane said her adopted mother told her that Faye went off. She said that her adopted mother told Faye that they could talk another time after she had calmed down. I couldn't help but to wonder if Faye ever told our father or her sister Lillian about this before she passed? Faye and Cheryl never had a good relationship, and this was just another reason for Faye to dislike her even more. From all accounts Faye was a loud woman who was not afraid to speak her truth. I could just imagine if she had found out about me. A match-up between her and my mother would have been epic.

Although we were total strangers I am glad that I can say that I did actually get to see and speak to my aunt. Maybe she's looking down on me and smiling about the truth finally coming out.

Aunt Lillian

Lillian was my father's oldest sister and Bobby's mother. She was born in March of 1931 in Gates County, North Carolina. Just like Faye, Lillian was probably also oblivious to the fact that I was her nephew. Although I have no memory of ever seeing or meeting her, it isn't impossible that I didn't.

I found out that Lillian had worked at Uniroyal for many years. I was very familiar with Uniroyal because my mother and grandmother both worked there until the factory closed its doors sometime in the early nineties. Many people from the Waterbury area worked at Uniroyal, which was located in Naugatuck, Connecticut. Knowing the environment at Uniroyal like I did; it was a very tight knit company where all the Black people knew each other. Many were migrants from the south and it was during a time when Black people stuck together more closely. It would have been highly unlikely that my mother or grandmother didn't know Lillian.

As I continued to put the pieces together it was becoming more and more obvious that my mother knew my father's family very well. I don't know if she did because she wanted to secretly keep tabs on him or because she was just genuinely friends with them. Knowing my mother, it was probably a little of both. I just find it amazing how she could be in these people's presence and keep such a secret from them.

Lillian also had a daughter, Carolyn, who had died prematurely in November of 1984 in Waterbury, Connecticut., This was two years after I had graduated from high school. I couldn't help but think of how many immediate family members I would never get the chance to meet due to this secret held by my mother for all these years. Fortunately, Bobby is still around, and we speak frequently. You can say every time we talk we are trying to catch up on lost time. I could definitely see him being someone that I would have hung around with when we were younger. I try not to be pushy for information from anyone because to them this is old history which could bring up bad memories, as for me everything I'm learning is new to me.

Unfortunately, Lillian passed away in September of 2012, one year after the death of my uncle Fred. If my uncle Fred were around I'm sure I could have gotten some answers out of him.

William's Women

It's easy to see where William may have gone wrong in his relationships, but to be fair the women he choose had their fair share of issues too. Maybe that's what attracted him to them or maybe he created them. That's a question we may never know the answer to.

There didn't seem to be a particular type of woman that William was attracted to. He definitely didn't discriminate. He had older women, younger women, short and tall women, women of different ethnicities. It didn't matter. I guess as long as they were women and good looking they were his type, but as he aged his women did become much younger than him.

I'll start with my mother. In some ways she was perfect. She didn't drink, swear, or hang out in the streets. She was a hard worker and was close to her family, but then there's the downside. My mother was known for her attitude and violent temper. She wasn't your typical loving mother, showering you with kisses and hugs and telling you how much she loves you.

She wasn't the type of mother who would throw parties for your birthday and invite your friends over to celebrate. To this day I have never had a birthday party nor has my mother ever said I love you to me. If she did it must have been under her breath. She never praised me but was always quick to show her disapproval of things. When my mother and stepfather moved out of my great grandmother's apartment, I don't know if her decision to let me stay with my great grandmother was her way of not having to deal with me or to honor my wishes. Either way I'm glad I stayed with my great grandmother.

My mother had two more children after me, a girl, and a boy. If the way their lives turned out was any indication of what could have been in store for me then I guess you could say God was looking out for me. Being with my great grandmother, grandmother, step grandfather and my uncle taught me a lot about my heritage and family history on my mother's side of the family. I wouldn't trade that for the world.

Diane's biological mother, Cheryl, was something different. Diane's biological mother's story had many similarities to my own mother, but she was unique in her own right. Diane also was fortunate to have had the adopted parents who raised her, as I had my grandparents, but old secrets would come back to haunt Diane's mother too. If Kim and Tracey's life are any indication of how Diane's life would have turned out with her biological mother then Diane probably would have grown up in a dysfunctional household marred with alcoholism and abuse.

Diane's start in life was the rockiest. She was conceived by two people in a rocky marriage who got divorced prior to Diane being born. The doctors thought Diane would have mental disabilities which would prohibit here from having a normal life. Diane's mother was suffering from her own depression and mental issues and then figuratively killed Diane off to protect the secret that her child had been born. Against all those odds Diane went on to become a beautiful woman that leads a great life. She is probably the strongest of all the siblings.

Tiffany's mother is more of a mystery to me. I didn't know her and only knew of her from what Tiffany had told me. According to Tiffany her mother was much younger than our father when they met. Supposedly our father lied about his age to her mother in order to attract her to him. During their short relationship Tiffany said her mother told her that he was mentally and physically abusive to her. It wasn't until one day when her mother returned home and saw a bruise on Tiffany's leg that she decided to leave our father and get a restraining order. According to Tiffany her mother said that our father told her that she was crying too much so he hit her on her leg. Although our father lived close by Tiffany said he never made any attempt to reach out to her. I assumed it was probably because of the restraining order but no one knows for sure. Tiffany seemed to hold some resentment towards our father for not reaching out to her and having a relationship.

After the split, Tiffany stated that her mother married a man who raised her like his own. Tiffany never elaborated on her relationship with her mother, but it didn't seem as if they saw eye to eye on things. Tiffany still resides in California, but her mother has since moved to Florida.

Darryl and Davids's mother, Dixie, seemed to be the one to whom our father was most attracted to. As I looked through old photos that our father had there were plenty of pictures of Dixie throughout the years. Although they had split up it appeared that they maintained a civil relationship. I believe this was done for the sake of their two boys and or his love of Dixie. Darryl seemed to be the closest to our father. He spent the most time with him and was there for him until his death. Darryl told me one of the last things our father said to him before he died was, "Don't come visit my gravesite. I'm not there." Even in the face of death our father remained strong.

Although I only spoke to Ave once I did learn a little about her mother from her. Darryl had told me that he remembered getting out of school one day and going to over to our father's home. When he arrived, our father was kicking Ave and her mother out. Apparently something had happened in their relationship and our father was ending it. Ave was young at the time and probably has no memory of it. The only thing Ave could tell me about her mother was that she was loud and had a big mouth. Unknown to Darryl, Ave and our father did keep in touch after the split.

Ave said our father didn't want her to visit him when he was sick because he didn't want her to see and remember him like that. Ave seemed to admire our father a lot and even wrote a beautiful piece about him in his funeral program. Although Ave's mother and our father were not together it didn't seem to affect how Ave felt about him.

When I finally found Keisha she told me she had a beautiful relationship with her mother. According to Keisha her mother was the sweetest, kindest person you would ever want to meet. She said her mother calls her daily just to check in on her. When her mother found out that her siblings had reached out to her she was happy for her. Hearing Keisha speak so highly of her mother makes me wonder what went wrong so fast between her and William. To say William was a complicated man would be an understatement.

According to Darryl our father married another woman, but I couldn't find any information on that marriage. He said the marriage didn't last long and they did not have any children. The only record I could find was a divorce for William in 1981. That would have been about the time that Ave was conceived. One thing about our father was he didn't waste any time finding a replacement when he was finished with a woman.

Adulthood

Although part of my life for so long was a big lie, things did turn out well for me. I learned many trades, became a professional motorcycle drag racer, retired after 26 years as a police officer, pursued a career in the trucking industry and became an author. A lot for a kid whose mother said he would never make it anywhere in life because of his temper.

As with any family there will be differences. Some family members you will get along with, others you won't and some you will tolerate just for the greater good. If I had the opportunity to change anything in my life would I? No! Would I add anything? Yes!

Prior to completing this book, I decided to take a ride through the old neighborhood where me and some of my siblings grew up. Let me tell you things don't look the same now. I mean a lot of the buildings are still there and the general layout is the same, but the memories have changed. Now when I drive by my sister's old home I remember seeing her either outside or going into her home totally unaware of her being my sister.

I drove past places where I remember running into my brother Tracey and being totally unaware of him being my brother. I drove past the old Berkely Heights Apartments where my grandmother, father, his sisters, and Bobby grew up and remembering the many times as a child that I had been to those apartments to visit family from my mother's side of the family. I drove past the house where my aunt Faye and her son Chad died in that horrible fire in 1994. I drove past the catholic school where my sister went and the high school where my father graduated. I drove past places where my father took some of the pictures that Darryl gave me. These are all old places that now have much more significant meaning to me now than they did before. Meanings that are real and not the false meanings that I once had before I found out the truth. I now feel as though my eyes have been opened and I have awakened.

Redemption

Redemption, whether in a moral, spiritual, social, or financial sense, involves a process of reclaiming something valuable that was lost or damaged, whether it be integrity, a relationship, one's standing in society, or even material wealth. It often requires effort, sacrifice, and a genuine desire to change or correct past wrong doings. For me it was a **personal transformation** where I sought to overcome the past, learn from mine and others' mistakes, and to become a better person.

For the first time in my life, I was able to shed the guilt associated with not knowing who my biological father was and the sense of rejection that came with feeling as though I had been abandoned by him. Finding my siblings and getting closure by visiting my biological father's gravesite was exactly what I needed to feel complete. Every day I'm a work in progress but I know that with each passing day I am a better person today than I was yesterday. As for my mother, that is a journey she will have to face alone.

Until she comes to terms with who she is and what she has done she may never be able to move forward with her life. In some ways she is still stuck in the sixties when she first met William and became pregnant by him. I often wondered if that is what drove me to be better, do better. Was I always running away from that label that was stuck on my back at birth? Maybe I wanted to prove that I could be something more so that my biological father could see me one day and see how successful I had become without his help. I don't know the answer and in the end I don't even know if it even matters. I became my own man and that is what I can take the credit for, the good and the bad.

As for my biological father and my family on his side, I do regret that they never got the opportunity to know the truth, to know me. They too were also cheated by my mother. She had no right to deny them the opportunity to know and have a relationship with me just because of her hatred for William. She can hate and blame William all she wants but she needs to remember that she too holds most of the blame.

We as siblings have a lot to catch up on seeing that we went decades without even knowing the others existed. My relationship with Tiffany is a little complicated. Although she was the one who initially contacted me on Ancestry to make me aware that I was her brother, when I made the trip to California to see her she stood me up. Up to that point we had talked and shared quite a bit of information. I don't know what happened, but my door is always open if she ever wants to talk or possibly meet in the future.

Darryl is my little bro. We play video billiards almost every day and I am constantly in touch with him or his wife Michelle daily. Darryl is funny and can be forgetful sometimes, but I love him just the same.

Diane is my go-to sister. She is the first sibling that I got to meet face to face. We're in touch with each other every day and we are always having some silly conversations. She lives the closest to me out of all the siblings, so I get to see her the most. I work a lot but when I'm available I get to spend time with her and her family. I even got to see the birth of my great nephew Carter. Now that's he's older he seems to get a kick out of dialing my number from Diane's phone. I think hearing a voice on the other end excites him.

Diane could spot a good man a mile away judging by her adopted father and husband. She told me about how her adopted father came to the orphanage with his wife and as soon as she saw him she put her hands in the air and said uppy. He picked her up and said, this is the one for me. Diane said he was a great father to her. The same applied to her husband. She said she hadn't been going out with him for that long when she told her adopted mother that she was going to marry him. That was thirty years ago this year, and they are still happily together.

Keisha is a sweetheart. She was the last one that I was able to locate but it was worth the work. Unlike most of our mothers her mother is very sweet and supportive. Keisha says her mother calls her every day and is always asking her about her relationship with her newfound siblings.

As for Tracey, David, and Ave there's not much that I can say about them. Maybe they need more time to process this, maybe they legitimately don't want to be bothered. Everyone goes through something different in life and maybe they are going through theirs. No matter what, they are still my siblings, and I would more than welcome them anytime whenever they are ready to talk.

Kim would have been the oldest of us all. Unfortunately, her life was cut short before any of us got a chance to know her. I can't help but to think of what kind of woman she would have been today. Unfortunately, none of us will ever get a chance to find out. I periodically go to the graveyard to pay my respects to her.

It's just a grim reminder of the fact that we have to live each day as if it were our last because we never know when our time is up.

Who knows what the future may hold. Maybe there will be a family reunion with us all one day or maybe a major motion picture will be made with an all-star cast depicting us, detailing the struggles that we endured and survived. If I learnt nothing else in life it is that life has endless possibilities, and you never know where it may take you. My search will always continue to find new clues and information about the family I never knew. In the end I found love, happiness and family and nothing is more important than that.

As of this writing my mother's health is failing and she still refuses to speak to me. At this point I don't even think I want her to. Unfortunately, I can't give back what was never given to me, compassion, honesty, and love. This is not the kind of relationship anyone should have with any parent, but it is the one that I was given. I'm at peace with myself and that is what I will have to live with.

About the Author

Andrew Abney was born to a single mother in Waterbury, CT at a time when being a single mother was harshly looked down upon in society. Although he had a good life it was merely an illusion covering up for the truth. Through faith and determination, he found the key to unlock the mystery of his past and reclaim his lost heritage. Faith can make anything possible.

Acknowledgments

First I have to dedicate this book to our sister that didn't make the journey with us, Kim. I wish she could have been here. Next I have to acknowledge the friends and family that made this book possible for me to share my life and theirs with the world, putting up with all my questions and taking the time to listen to me. I also can't forget the people who picked up this book and decided to read it. Hopefully, my story can help others.

www.ingramcontent.com/pod-product-compliance
Lightning Source LLC
Chambersburg PA
CBHW070205160726
47997CB00017B/250